The letters of Fabius, in 1788, on the Federal Constitution; and in 1797, on the present situation of public affairs. Copy-right secured.

John Dickinson

The letters of Fabius, in 1788, on the Federal Constitution; and in 1797, on the present situation of public affairs. Copy-right secured.

Dickinson, John

ESTCID: W021264

Reproduction from Library of Congress

Attributed to John Dickinson in the Dictionary of American biography. "The first nine letters in this collection, published in the beginning of the year 1788 .. appeared separately in news-papers; and have never been published together, before the present edition."--p. iii. "Errata."--p. [203].

[Wilmington, Del.] : From the office of the Delaware gazette, Wilmington, by W.C. Smyth, 1797.

iv,202,[2]p. ; 22 cm

Gale ECCO Print Editions

Relive history with *Eighteenth Century Collections Online*, now available in print for the independent historian and collector. This series includes the most significant English-language and foreign-language works printed in Great Britain during the eighteenth century, and is organized in seven different subject areas including literature and language; medicine, science, and technology; and religion and philosophy. The collection also includes thousands of important works from the Americas.

The eighteenth century has been called "The Age of Enlightenment." It was a period of rapid advance in print culture and publishing, in world exploration, and in the rapid growth of science and technology – all of which had a profound impact on the political and cultural landscape. At the end of the century the American Revolution, French Revolution and Industrial Revolution, perhaps three of the most significant events in modern history, set in motion developments that eventually dominated world political, economic, and social life.

In a groundbreaking effort, Gale initiated a revolution of its own: digitization of epic proportions to preserve these invaluable works in the largest online archive of its kind. Contributions from major world libraries constitute over 175,000 original printed works. Scanned images of the actual pages, rather than transcriptions, recreate the works *as they first appeared.*

Now for the first time, these high-quality digital scans of original works are available via print-on-demand, making them readily accessible to libraries, students, independent scholars, and readers of all ages.

For our initial release we have created seven robust collections to form one the world's most comprehensive catalogs of 18th century works.

Initial Gale ECCO Print Editions collections include:

History and Geography

Rich in titles on English life and social history, this collection spans the world as it was known to eighteenth-century historians and explorers. Titles include a wealth of travel accounts and diaries, histories of nations from throughout the world, and maps and charts of a world that was still being discovered. Students of the War of American Independence will find fascinating accounts from the British side of conflict.

Social Science

Delve into what it was like to live during the eighteenth century by reading the first-hand accounts of everyday people, including city dwellers and farmers, businessmen and bankers, artisans and merchants, artists and their patrons, politicians and their constituents. Original texts make the American, French, and Industrial revolutions vividly contemporary.

Medicine, Science and Technology

Medical theory and practice of the 1700s developed rapidly, as is evidenced by the extensive collection, which includes descriptions of diseases, their conditions, and treatments. Books on science and technology, agriculture, military technology, natural philosophy, even cookbooks, are all contained here.

Literature and Language

Western literary study flows out of eighteenth-century works by Alexander Pope, Daniel Defoe, Henry Fielding, Frances Burney, Denis Diderot, Johann Gottfried Herder, Johann Wolfgang von Goethe, and others. Experience the birth of the modern novel, or compare the development of language using dictionaries and grammar discourses.

Religion and Philosophy

The Age of Enlightenment profoundly enriched religious and philosophical understanding and continues to influence present-day thinking. Works collected here include masterpieces by David Hume, Immanuel Kant, and Jean-Jacques Rousseau, as well as religious sermons and moral debates on the issues of the day, such as the slave trade. The Age of Reason saw conflict between Protestantism and Catholicism transformed into one between faith and logic -- a debate that continues in the twenty-first century.

Law and Reference

This collection reveals the history of English common law and Empire law in a vastly changing world of British expansion. Dominating the legal field is the *Commentaries of the Law of England* by Sir William Blackstone, which first appeared in 1765. Reference works such as almanacs and catalogues continue to educate us by revealing the day-to-day workings of society.

Fine Arts

The eighteenth-century fascination with Greek and Roman antiquity followed the systematic excavation of the ruins at Pompeii and Herculaneum in southern Italy; and after 1750 a neoclassical style dominated all artistic fields. The titles here trace developments in mostly English-language works on painting, sculpture, architecture, music, theater, and other disciplines. Instructional works on musical instruments, catalogs of art objects, comic operas, and more are also included.

The BiblioLife Network

This project was made possible in part by the BiblioLife Network (BLN), a project aimed at addressing some of the huge challenges facing book preservationists around the world. The BLN includes libraries, library networks, archives, subject matter experts, online communities and library service providers. We believe every book ever published should be available as a high-quality print reproduction; printed on-demand anywhere in the world. This insures the ongoing accessibility of the content and helps generate sustainable revenue for the libraries and organizations that work to preserve these important materials.

The following book is in the "public domain" and represents an authentic reproduction of the text as printed by the original publisher. While we have attempted to accurately maintain the integrity of the original work, there are sometimes problems with the original work or the micro-film from which the books were digitized. This can result in minor errors in reproduction. Possible imperfections include missing and blurred pages, poor pictures, markings and other reproduction issues beyond our control. Because this work is culturally important, we have made it available as part of our commitment to protecting, preserving, and promoting the world's literature.

GUIDE TO FOLD-OUTS MAPS and OVERSIZED IMAGES

The book you are reading was digitized from microfilm captured over the past thirty to forty years. Years after the creation of the original microfilm, the book was converted to digital files and made available in an online database.

In an online database, page images do not need to conform to the size restrictions found in a printed book. When converting these images back into a printed bound book, the page sizes are standardized in ways that maintain the detail of the original. For large images, such as fold-out maps, the original page image is split into two or more pages

Guidelines used to determine how to split the page image follows:

• Some images are split vertically; large images require vertical and horizontal splits.
• For horizontal splits, the content is split left to right.
• For vertical splits, the content is split from top to bottom.
• For both vertical and horizontal splits, the image is processed from top left to bottom right.

THE
LETTERS

OF *Sam. H. Smith* [handwritten]

FABIUS,

"ps. John Dickinson [handwritten]

IN 1788,

ON THE FEDERAL CONSTITUTION;

AND

IN 1797,

ON THE PRESENT SITUATION

OF

PUBLIC AFFAIRS.

———

Copy-Right Secured.

———

FROM THE OFFICE OF THE DELAWARE
GAZETTE, WILMINGTON,
BY W. C. SMYTH.

1797.

The EDITOR to the PUBLIC.

THE firſt Nine Letters in this Collection, publiſhed in the beginning of the Year 1788, were occaſioned by an alarming heſitation of ſome States to ratify the Conſtitution propoſed by the Federal Convention in 1787.

They appeared ſeparately in News-papers; and have never been publiſhed together, before the preſent Edition.

Some Notes are added of Extracts from " THE RIGHTS OF MAN," publiſhed about three Years after theſe Letters, containing ſimilar ſentiments, expreſſed with a remarkable reſemblance of Language, eſpecially on the two great ſubjects—the ORGANIZATION of a CONSTITUTION from *original* rights, and the FORMATION of GOVERNMENT from *contributed* rights, both of ſo much importance in laying regular FOUNDATIONS of Civil Society, and conſequently in ſecuring the advancement of HUMAN HAPPINESS.

The laſt ſet of Letters was cauſed by the extraordinary call of Congreſs, on the 25th Day of March, 1797.

Delaware } *to wit.*   (No. 2.)
District. }

BE IT REMEMBERED,
That on the twentieth day of September, in
the twenty-second year of the Independence of
the United States of America, *William Cather-
wood Smyth*, of the said district, hath deposited
in this Office, the Title of a Book, the Right
whereof he claims as Proprietor, in the words
following : to wit. " THE LETTERS OF
FABIUS, IN 1788, ON THE FEDERAL
CONSTITUTION, AND IN 1797, ON THE
PRESENT SITUATION OF PUBLIC AF-
FAIRS." In conformity to the Act of the
Congress of The United States, intitled, " An
Act for the encouragement of Learning," by
securing the Copies of Maps, Charts, and
Books, to the Authors, and to Proprietors of
such Copies, during the times therein menti-
oned.

JOHN CONWAY, Clk.
Delaware District.

I DO CERTIFY, that the above
is a true Copy of the Record thereof, as remaining of Record. IN
TESTIMONY whereof, I have
hereto set my hand, and affixed
the seal of the District aforesaid, on
the Day and Year first mentioned,
in the above Copy.

[L. S.]

JOHN CONWAY, Clk.
Delaware District.

THE
LETTERS
OF
FABIUS:
CONTAINING,
OBSERVATIONS on the CONSTITUTION
PROPOSED BY THE
FEDERAL CONVENTION.

LETTER I.

THE Conftitution propofed by the Federal Convention now engages the fixed attention of *America.*

Every perfon appears to be affected. Thofe who wifh the adoption of the plan, confider its rejection as the fource of endlefs contefts, confufions, and misfortunes; and they alfo confider a refolution to alter, without previoufly adopting it, as a rejection.

Thofe who oppofe the plan, are influenced by different views. Some of them are friends, others of them are enemies, to *The United States.*

A

The latter are of two claffes; either men without principles or fortunes, who think they may
have a chance to mend their circumftances,
with impunity, under a *weak government*, or in
public convulfions, but cannot make them worfe
even by the laft—or men who have been always averfe to the revolution; and though at
firft confounded by that event, yet, their hopes
reviving with the declenfion of our affairs, have
fince perfuaded themfelves, that at length the
people, tired out with their continued diftreffes,
will return to their former connection with
Great Britain. To argue with thefe oppofers,
would be vain—The other oppofers of the plan
deferve the higheft refpect.

WHAT CONCERNS ALL, SHOULD BE CON-
SIDERED BY ALL; and individuals may injure
a whole fociety, by not declaring their fentiments. It is therefore not only their *right*, but
their *duty*, to declare them. Weak advocates
of a good caufe or artful advocates of a bad
one, may endeavour to ftop fuch communications, or to difcredit them by clamour and ca-
lumny. This, however, is not the age for
fuch tricks of controverfy. Men have fuffered
fo feverely by being deceived upon fubjects of
the higheft import, thofe of *religion* and *freedom*, that TRUTH becomes infinitely valuable
to them, not as a matter of curious fpeculation,
but of beneficial practice—A fpirit of inquiry
is excited, information diffufed, judgment
ftrengthened.

Before this tribunal of THE PEOPLE, let
every one freely fpeak, what he really thinks,

but with fo fincere a reverence for the caufe he ventures to difcufs, as to ufe the utmoft caution, left he fhould lead any into errors, upon a point of fuch facred concern as *the public happinefs.*

It is not the defign of this addrefs, to defcribe the prefent derangement of our affairs, the mifchiefs that muft enfue from its continuance, the horrors of a total diffolution of the union, or of the divifion of it into partial confederacies. Nor is it intended to defcribe the evils that will refult from purfuing the plan of another Federal Convention; as if a better temper of conciliation, or a more fatisfactory harmony of decifions, could be expected from men, after their minds are agitated with difgufts and difappointments, than before they were thus difturbed; though from an uncontradicted affertion it appears, that without fuch provocations, the difficulty of reconciling the interefts of the feveral ftates was fo near to INSUPERABLE, in the late convention, that after many weeks fpent in the moft faithful labours to promote concord, the members were upon the very point of difperfing in the utmoft diforder, jealoufy and refentment, and leaving the ftates expofed to all the tempefts of paffions, that have been fo fatal to confederacies of republics.

All thefe things, with obfervations on particular articles of the conftitution, have been laid before the public, and the writer of this addrefs means not to repeat what has been already faid. What he wifhes, is to *fimplify*

A 2

the fubject, fo as to facilitate the inquiries of his fellow citizens.

Many are the objections made to the fyftem propofed. They fhould be diftinguifhed. Some may be called *local*, becaufe they fpring from the fuppofed interefts of individual ftates. Thus, for inftance, fome inhabitants of large ftates may defire the fyftem to be fo altered, that they may poffefs more authority in the decifions of the government; or fome inhabitants of commercial ftates may defire it to be fo altered, that the advantages of trade may center almoft wholly among themfelves; and this predilection they may think compatible with the common welfare. Their judgment being thus warp'd, at the beginning of their deliberations, objections are accumulated as very important, that, without this prepoffeffion, would never have obtained their approbation. Certain it is, that ftrong underftandings may be fo influenced by this infulated patriotifm, as to doubt—whether general benefits can be communicated by a general government.*

Probably nothing would operate fo much for the correction of thefe errors, as the perufal of the accounts tranfmitted to us by the ancients, of the calamities occafioned in *Greece* by a conduct founded on fimilar miftakes. They are expreffly afcribed to this caufe—*that each city meditated a part on its own profit and ends——infomuch that thofe* WHO SEEMED TO CONTEND FOR UNION, *could never relinquifh their own in-*

---

* See fome late publications.

terefts and advancement, while they deliberated for the public.

Heaven grant! that our countrymen may pauſe in time—duly eſtimate the preſent moment—and ſolemnly reflect—whether their meaſures may not tend to draw down the ſame diſtractions upon us, that deſolated *Greece.*

They may now tolerably judge from the proceedings of the Federal Convention and of other conventions, what are the ſentiments of *America* upon her preſent and future proſpects. Let the voice of her diſtreſs be venerated—and adhering to the generous *Virginian* declaration, let them reſolve to " CLING TO UNION AS THE POLITICAL ROCK OF OUR SALVATION."

FABIUS.

Philadelphia,
April 10, 1788.

LETTER II.

BUT befides the objections originating from the before mentioned caufe, that have been called *local*, there are other objections that are fuppofed to arife from *maxims of liberty and policy*.——

Hence it is inferred, that the propofed fyftem has fuch inherent vices, as muft neceffarily produce a bad adminiftration, and at length the oppreffion of a monarchy and ariftocracy in the federal officers.

The writer of this addrefs being convinced by as exact an inveftigation as he could make, that fuch miftakes may lead to the perdition of his country, efteems it his indifpenfable duty, ftrenuoufly to contend, that—THE POWER OF THE PEOPLE pervading the propofed fyftem, together with the STRONG CONFEDERATION OF THE STATES, forms an adequate fecurity againft *every* danger that has been apprehended.

If this fingle affertion can be fupported by facts and arguments, there will be reafon to hope, that anxieties will be removed from the minds of fome citizens, who are truly devoted to the interefts of *America,* and who have been thrown into perplexities, by the mazes of multiplied and intricate difquifitions.

The objectors agree, that the *confederation of the ftates will be ftrong*, according to the fyftem propofed, and *fo ftrong*, that many of them loudly complain of that ftrength. On this part of the affertion, there is no difpute: But fome of the objections that have been publifhed,

ftrike at another part of the principle affumed,
and deny, that the fyftem is fufficiently founded on *the power of the people.*

The courfe of regular inquiry demands, that
thefe objections fhould be confidered in the firft
place. If *they* are removed, then *all the reft* of
the objections, concerning unneceffary taxa-
tions, ftanding armies, the abolifhment of trial by jury, the liberty of the prefs, the freedom of commerce, the judicial, executive, and
legiflative authorities of the feveral ftates, and
the rights of citizens, and the other abufes of
federal government, muft, of confequence, be
rejected, if the principle contains the falutary,
purifying, and preferving qualities attributed
to it. The queftion then will be—*Not what
may be done, when the government fhall be turned
into a tyranny; but how the government can be fo
turned?*

Thus unembarraffed by fubordinate difcuf-
fions, we may come fairly to the contempla-
tion of *that* fuperior point, and be better enabled to difcover, whether our attention to it
will afford any lights, whereby we may be
conducted to *peace, liberty,* and *fafety.*

The objections, denying that the fyftem propofed is fufficiently founded on *the power of the
people,* ftate, that the *number* of the federal truftees or officers, is too *fmall,* and that they are
to hold their *offices too long.*

One would really have fuppofed, that *fmall-
nefs of number* could not be termed a caufe of
danger, as *influence* muft increafe with *enlarge-
ment.* If this is a fault, it will foon be cor-

rected, as an addition will be often made to the number of the *fenators*, and, a much greater and more frequently, to that of the *reprefenta-tives*; and in all probability much fooner, than we fhall be able and willing to bear the ex-pence of the addition.

As to the *fenate*, it never can be, and it ne-ver ought to be large, if it is to poffefs the powers, which almoft all the objectors feem inclined to allot to it, as will be evident to every intelligent perfon, who confiders thofe powers.

Though fmall, let it be remembered, that it is to be created by the *fovereignties* of the feve-ral ftates; that is, by the perfons, whom *the people* of each ftate fhall judge to be *moft worthy*, and who, furely, will be religioufly attentive to making a felection, in which the intereft and honour of their ftate will be fo deeply concerned. It fhould be remembered too, that this is *the fame manner*, in which the members of Con-grefs are *now* appointed; and that *herein*, the *fovereignties* of the ftates are fo intimately in-volved, that however a *renunciation* of part of thefe powers may be defired by *fome of the ftates*, it NEVER will be obtained from *the reft* of them. Peaceable, fraternal, and benevolent as *thefe* are, they think, the conceffions *they* have made, ought to fatisfy *all*.

That the *fenate* may always be kept *full*, with-out the interference of Congrefs, it is provided in the fyftem, that if vacancies happen by re-fignation or otherwife, during the recefs of the legiflature of any ftate, the executive thereof may make temporary appointments, until the next meeting of the legiflature, which *fhall* then fill up fuch vacancies.

As *to the houfe of reprefentatives*, it is to confift of a number of perfons, not exceeding one for every thirty thoufand: But each ftate fhall have at leaft one reprefentative. The electors will refide, widely difperfed, over an extenfive country. Cabal and corruption will be as impracticable, as, on fuch occafions, human inftitutions can render them. *The will of freemen,* thus circumftanced, will give the *fiat.* The purity of election thus obtained, will amply compenfate for the fuppofed defect of reprefentation; and the members, *thus chofen,* will be moft apt to harmonize in their proceedings, with *the general* interefts, feelings, and fentiments of the people.

Allowing fuch an increafe of population as, from experience and a variety of caufes, may be expected, the *reprefentatives,* in a fhort period, will amount to feveral hundreds, and moft probably long before any change of manners for the worfe, that might tempt or encourage our rulers to mal-adminiftration, will take place on this continent.

That *this houfe* may *always* be kept *full*, without the interference of Congrefs, it is provided in the fyftem, that when vacancies happen in any ftate, the executive authority thereof *fhall* iffue writs of election to fill fuch vacancies.

But, it feems, the number of the federal officers is not only too fmall: They are to hold their offices *too long.*

B

This objection surely applies not to *the house of representatives*, who are to be chosen *every two years*, especially if the extent of empire, and the vast variety and importance of their deliberations, be considered. In that view, *they* and *the senate* will actually be not only *legislative* but also *diplomatic* bodies, perpetually engaged in the arduous task of reconciling, in their determinations, the interests of several *sovereign* states, not to insist on the necessity of a competent knowledge of *foreign* affairs, relative to the states.

They who desire the *representatives* to be chosen *every year*, should exceed *Newton* in calculations, if they attempt to evince, that the public business would, in that case, be better transacted, than when they are chosen *every two years*. The idea, however, should be excused for the zeal that prompted it.

Is monarchy or aristocracy to be produced, without the consent of the people, by a *house of representatives*, thus constituted?

It has been unanimously agreed by the friends of liberty, that FREQUENT ELECTIONS OF THE REPRESENTATIVES OF THE PEOPLE, ARE THE SOVEREIGN REMEDY OF ALL GRIEVANCES IN A FREE GOVERNMENT.— Let us pass on to the senate.

At the end of two years after the first election, *one third* is to be elected for *six* years; and at the end of *four* years, another third. Thus one third will constantly have but *four* years, and another but *two* years to continue in office. The whole number at first will amount to *twenty-fix*, will be regularly *renovated* by the *biennial* election of *one third*, and will be *over-looked, and overawed* by the houfe of *reprefenta-tives*, nearly three times more numerous at the beginning, rapidly and vaftly augmenting, and more enabled to overlook and overawe them, by holding *their* offices for *two* years, as thereby they will acquire better information, refpecting national affairs. Thefe *reprefentatives* will alfo command the public purfe, as *all* bills *for raif-ing revenue*, muft *originate* in their houfe.

As in the *Roman* armies, when the *Principes* and *Haftati* had failed, there were ftill the *Tri-arii*, who generally put things to rights, fo we fhall be fupplied with another refource.

We are to have a *prefident*, to *fuperintend*, and if he thinks the public weal requires it, *to con-troul* any act of the *reprefentatives* and *fenate*.

This prefident is to be chofen, not by the people at large, becaufe it may not be poffible, that all the freemen of the empire fhould always have the neceffary information, for directing their choice of fuch an officer; nor by Con-grefs, left it fhould difturb the national coun-cils; nor BY ANY ONE STANDING BODY WHATEVER, for fear of undue influence.

He is to be chofen in the following manner. Each ftate fhall appoint, as the legiflature there-of may direct, a number of *electors*, equal to *the whole number of fenators and reprefentatives*, to which the ftate fhall be entitled in Congrefs: but no *fenator* or *reprefentative*, or *perfon holding an office of truft or profit under the United States*, fhall be appointed an elector. As thefe electors are to be appointed, as the legiflature of each ftate may direct, the faireft, freeft opening is given, for each ftate to chufe fuch *electors* for this purpofe, as fhall be moft fignally qualified to fulfil the truft.

To guard againft undue influence thefe electors, thus chofen, are to meet *in their refpective ftates*, and vote *by ballot;* and ftill further to guard againft it, Congrefs may determine the *time of chufing the electors, and the days on which they fhall give their votes*—WHICH DAY SHALL BE THE SAME THROUGHOUT THE UNITED STATES. All the votes from the feveral ftates are to be tranfmitted to Congrefs, and therein counted. The prefident is to hold his office for *four* years.

When thefe electors meet in their refpective ftates, utterly vain will be the unreafonable fuggeftions derived from *partiality.* The electors may throw away their votes, mark, with public difappointment, fome perfon improperly favoured by them, or juftly revering the duties of their office, dedicate their votes to the beft interefts of their country.

This prefident will be no dictator. *Two thirds of the reprefentatives* and *the fenate* may pafs any law, *notwithftanding his diffent;* and he is *removable* and *punifhable* for mifbehaviour.

Can this limited, fluctuating *fenate,* placed amidft fuch powers, if it fhould become willing, ever become able, to make *America* pafs under its yoke? The fenators will generally be inhabitants of places very diftant one from another. They can fcarcely be acquainted till they meet. Few of them can ever act together for any length of time, unlefs their good conduct recommends them to a re-election; and then there will be frequent changes in a body *dependant upon the acts of other bodies*, the legiflatures of the feveral ftates, that are altering every year. *Machiavel* and *Cæfar Borgia* together could not form a confpiracy in fuch a fenate, deftructive to any but themfelves and their accomplices.

It is effential to every good government, that there fhould be *fome council*, permanent enough to get a due *knowledge* of affairs internal and external; fo conftituted, that by fome deaths or removals, the current of *information* fhould not be impeded or difturbed; and fo regulated, as to be refponfible to, and controulable *by the people*. Where can the authority for combining thefe advantages, be more *fafely*, *beneficially*, or *fatisfactorily* lodged, than in the fenate, to be formed according to the plan propofed? Shall parts of the truft be committed to the prefident, with *counfellors* who fhall fubfcribe their advices?* If affaults upon liberty are to be guarded againft, and furely they ought to be with fleeplefs vigilance, why fhould we depend more on *the commander in chief* of the army and navy of *The United States*, and of the militia of the feveral ftates, and on *his* counfellors, whom he may fecretly influence, than on the *fenate* to be appointed by the perfons exercifing the *fovereign* authority of the feveral ftates? In truth, th

---

* *See late publications.*

objections againſt the powers of the ſenate originated from a deſire to have them, or at leaſt
ſome of them, veſted in a body, in which
the ſeveral ſtates ſhould be repreſented, in proportion to the number of inhabitants, as in the
houſe of repreſentatives. This method is UN-
ATTAINABLE, and the wiſh for it ſhould be
diſmiſſed from every mind, that deſires the exiſtence of a confederation.

What aſſurance can be given, or what probability be aſſigned, that a board of *counſellors*
would continue honeſt, longer than the *ſenate?*
Or, that they would poſſeſs more uſeful information, reſpecting all the ſtates, than the ſe-
nators of all the ſtates? It appears needleſs to
purſue this argument any further.

How varied, balanced, concordant, and benign, is the ſyſtem propoſed to us? To ſecure
the freedom, and promote the happineſs of
theſe and future ſtates, by giving THE WILL
OF THE PEOPLE a deciſive influence over the
whole, and over all the parts, with what a
comprehenſive arrangement does it embrace
different modes of repreſentation, from an
election by a county to an election by an empire? What are the complicated ballot, and all
the refined devices of *Venice* for maintaining
her ariſtocracy, when compared with this plain-
dealing work for diffuſing the bleſſings of *equal
liberty and common proſperity* over myriads of the
human race?

All the foundations before mentioned, of the
federal government, are by the propoſed ſyſtem
to be eſtabliſhed, in the moſt clear, ſtrong,

pofitive, unequivocal expreſſions, of which our language is capable. *Magna charta*, or any other law, never contained clauſes more deciſive and emphatic. While the people of theſe ſtates have ſenſe, they will underſtand them; and while they have ſpirit, they will make them to be obſerved.

FABIUS.

LETTER III.

THE writer of this addrefs hopes, that he will now be thought fo difengaged from the objections againſt the principle aſſumed, that he may be excuſed for recurring to his aſſertion, that—*the power of the people* pervading the propoſed fyſtem, together with *the ſtrong confederation of the ſtates*, will form an adequate fecurity againſt *every* danger that has been apprehended.

It is a mournful, but may be a uſeful truth, that the liberty of *ſingle republics* has generally been deſtroyed by *ſome of the citizens*, and of *confederated republics*, by *ſome of the aſſociated ſtates.*

It is more pleaſing, and may be more profitable to reflect, that, their tranquility and profperity have commonly been promoted, in proportion to the ſtrength of their government for protecting *the worthy* againſt *the licentious.*

As in forming a political fociety, *each* individual *contributes* ſome of his rights, in order that *he* may, from A COMMON STOCK of rights, derive *greater benefits*, than he could from merely HIS OWN; fo, in forming a confederation, each political fociety ſhould *contribute* ſuch a ſhare of their rights, as will, from A COMMON STOCK of *theſe* rights, produce the largeſt quantity of benefits for *them.*

But, *what is that ſhare?* and, *how to be managed?* Momentous queſtions! Here, flattery is treaſon; and error, deſtruction.

Are they unanfwerable ? No. Our moft gracious CREATOR does not *condemn* us to figh for unattainable bleffednefs : But one thing he *demands*—that we fhould feek for happinefs in *his* way, and not in *our own*.

Humility and *benevolence* muft take place of *pride* and *overweening felfifhnefs*. Reafon, rifing above thefe mifts, will then difcover to us, that we cannot be true to ourfelves, without being true to others—that to love our neighbours as ourfelves, is to love ourfelves in the beft manner—that to give, is to gain—and, that we never confult our own happinefs more effectually, than when we moft endeavour to correfpond with THE DIVINE DESIGNS, by communicating happinefs, as much as we can, to our fellow-creatures. INESTIMABLE TRUTH ! fufficient, if they do not barely afk what it is, to melt tyrants into men, and to foothe the inflamed minds of a multitude into mildnefs—INESTIMABLE TRUTH! which our Maker in his providence, enables us, not only to talk and write about, but to adopt in practice of vaft extent, and of inftructive example.

Let us now enquire, if there be not fome PRINCIPLE, *fimple as the laws of nature* in other inftances, from which, as from a SOURCE, the many benefits of fociety are deduced.

We may with reverence fay, that our CREATOR defigned *men* for fociety, becaufe otherwife they cannot be happy. They cannot be happy without freedom ; nor free without fecurity ; that is, without the *abfence of fear* ; nor thus fecure, without fociety. The conclufion is ftrictly fyllogiftic—that men cannot be free without fociety. Of courfe, they cannot be *equally free* without fociety, WHICH FREEDOM PRODUCES THE GREATEST HAPPINESS.

As thefe premifes are invincible, we have advanced a confiderable way in our enquiry upon THIS DEEPLY INTERESTING SUBJECT. If we can determine, what fhare of his rights, every individual muft contribute to THE COMMON STOCK of rights in forming a fociety, for obtaining *equal freedom*, we determine at the fame time, what fhare of their rights each political fociety muft contribute to THE COMMON STOCK of rights in forming a confederation, which is only a larger fociety, for obtaining *equal freedom:* For, if the depofite be not proportioned to the magnitude of the affociation in the latter cafe, it will generate the fame mifchief among the component parts of it, from their inequality, that would refult from a defective contribution to affociation in the former cafe, among the component parts of it, from their inequality.

Each individual then muft contribute fuch a fhare of his rights, as is neceffary for attaining that SECURITY that is effential to freedom; and he is bound to make this contribution by the law of his nature, which prompts him to a participated happinefs; that is, by the command of his creator; therefore, *he muft fubmit his will,* IN WHAT CONCERNS ALL, *to the will of all, that is of the whole fociety.* What does he lofe by this fubmiffion? The power of doing

injuries to others—and the dread of suffering
injuries from them. What does he gain by it?
The aid of those associated with him, for his
relief from the incommodities of mental or bo-
dily weakness—the pleasure for which his heart
is formed—of doing good—PROTECTION
against injuries—a capacity of enjoying his
undelegated rights to the best advantage—a re-
peal of his fears—and tranquility of mind—
or, in other words, that *perfect liberty* better
described in the Holy Scriptures, than any
where else, in these expressions—" When *every*
man shall *sit* under his vine, and under his fig-
tree, and NONE SHALL MAKE HIM AFRAID."
The like submission, with a correspondent
expansion and accommodation, must be made
between *states*, for obtaining the like benefits
in a *confederation*. MEN are the materials of
both. As the largest number is but a junction
of UNITS—a confederation is but an assemblage
of *individuals*. The auspicious influence of
that *law* of his nature, upon which the happiness of MAN depends in society, must attend
him in confederation, or he becomes unhappy;
for confederation should promote the happiness
of *individuals*, or it does not ANSWER THE IN-
TENDED PURPOSE. Herein there is a progres-
sion, not a contradiction. As MAN, he becomes a *citizen*; as a citizen, he becomes a
federalist. The generation of one, *is not the destruction* of the other. He *carries* into society
his naked rights: *These* thereby improved, he
carries still forward into confederation. If
that sacred law before mentioned, is not here

obſerved, the confederation would not be *real*, but *pretended*. He would confide, and be deceived.*

---

* " *The error of thoſe who reaſon by precedent, drawn from antiquity, reſpecting* the rights of man, *is, that they do not go far enough into antiquity. They do not go the whole way. They ſtop in ſome of the intermediate ſtages of an hundred or a thouſand years, and produce what was then done, as a rule for the preſent day. This is no authority at all. If we travel ſtill further into antiquity, we ſhall find a direct contrary opinion and practice prevailing; and if antiquity is to be authority, a thouſand ſuch authorities may be produced, ſucceſſively contradicting each other: but if we proceed on, at laſt we ſhall come out right: We ſhall then come to the time when man came from the hand of his Maker. What was he then?* MAN. *Man was his high and only title, and a higher cannot be given him———We are now got at the origin of man, and at* the origin of his rights.——— *Every hiſtory of the creation, and every traditionary account, whether from the lettered or unlettered world, however they may vary in their opinion or belief of certain particulars, all agree in eſtabliſhing one point, the* UNITY *of man; by which* I *mean that man is all of* one degree, *and conſequently that all men are born equal, and with* equal natural rights. *By conſidering man in this light, it* places him in a cloſe connection with all his duties, *whether to his* CREATOR, *or to the* creation, *of which he is a part; and it is only where he forgets his* ORIGIN, *or, to uſe a more faſhion-*

The dilemma is inevitable. There muft either be *one* will, or *feveral* wills. If but *one* will, *all* the people are concerned; if *feveral* wills, *few* comparatively are concerned. Surprizing! that this doctrine fhould be contended for by thofe, who declare, that the conftitution is not founded on a *bottom broad enough;* and, though THE WHOLE PEOPLE of The United States are to be TREBLY reprefented in it in THREE DIFFERENT MODES of reprefentation, and their fervants will have the moft advantageous fituations and opportunities of acquiring all requifite information for the welfare of *the*

---

able phrafe, his birth and family, that he becomes diffolute.

Hitherto we have fpoken only (and that but in part) of the natural *rights of man. We have now to confider the* civil *rights of man, and to fhew how the one* ORIGINATES *out of the other.—— Man did not enter into* fociety, *to become* worfe *than he was before, nor to have lefs rights than he had before, but to have thofe rights* BETTER SECURED. *His* natural *rights are the foundation of all his* civil *rights. But in order to purfue this diftinction with more precifion, it will be neceffary to mark the different qualities of* natural *and* civil *rights.*

A few words will explain this. Natural rights are thofe which appertain to man in right of his exiftence—civil rights are thofe which appertain to man in right of his being a member of fociety. Every civil right has for its foundation fome natural right pre-exifting in the individual, but

whole union, yet infift for a privilege of *oppofing*, *obftructing*, and *confounding* all their meafures taken with common confent for the general weal, by the delays, negligences, rivalries, or other felfifh views of *parts* of the union.

Thus, while one ftate fhould be relied upon by the union for giving aid, upon a recommendation of Congrefs, to another in diftrefs, the latter might be ruined; and the ftate relied upon, might fuppofe, it would gain by fuch an event.

When any perfons fpeak of a confideration, do they, or do they not acknowledge, that the *whole* is *interefted* in the fafety of *every* part—in the *agreement* of *parts*—in the *relation* of *parts*

---

to unite his individual power is not, in all cafes, fufficiently competent. Of this kind are all thofe which relate to SECURITY *and* PROTECTION.

From this fhort review it will be eafy to diftinguifh between that clafs of natural rights which man retains after entering into fociety, and thofe which he throws into COMMON STOCK *as a member of fociety. The natural rights which he retains, are all thofe in which the power to execute is as perfect in the individual as the right itfelf.— The natural rights which are not retained, are all thofe in which, though the right is perfect in the individual, the power to execute them is defective:* THEY ANSWER NOT HIS PURPOSE—*thofe he* DEPOSITS *in the* COMMON STOCK *of fociety, and takes the arm of fociety, of which he is a part, in preference and in addition to his own. Society grants him nothing. Every man is a proprietor in fociety, and draws on the capital as a matter of right."*

Rights of Man, 1791. *page* 30, 31.

to *one another—to the whole*—or, to *other focie-ties?* If they do—then, the *authority* of the *whole*, muft be co-extenfive with its *interefts*—and if it is, the *will of the whole* muft and *ought* in *fuch cafes* to govern ; or elfe *the whole* would have interefts without an authority to manage them—a pofition which prejudice it-felf cannot digeft.

If they do not acknowledge, that *the whole is thus interefted*, the converfation fhould ceafe. Such perfons mean not a confederation, but fomething elfe.

As to the idea, that *this fuperintending fove-reign will* muft of confequence deftroy the fub-ordinate fovereignties of the feveral ftates, it is begging a conceffion of the queftion, by infer-ring, that a manifeft and great *ufefulnefs* muft neceffarily end in *abufe ;* and not only fo, but it requires an extinction of *the principle of all fociety :* for, the fubordinate fovereignties, or, in other words, the *undelegated rights* of the feveral *ftates,* in a *confederation,* ftand upon the very fame foundation with the *undelegated rights* of *individuals* in a *fociety,* the *federal fovereign will* being *compofed* of the *fubordinate fovereign wills* of the feveral confederated ftates. As fome perfons feem to think, *a bill of rights* is *the beft fecurity* of rights, the *fovereignties* of the feve-ral ftates have *this* beft fecurity by the propofed conftitution, and *more than this* beft fecurity, for *they* are not barely *declared* to be rights, but are taken into it as *component parts* for *their* per-petual prefervation—by *themfelves.* In fhort, the government of each ftate is, and is to be, *sovereign* and *supreme* in *all* matters that *relate* to each ftate *only*. It is to be *subordinate* barely in *those* matters that *relate* to *the whole;* and it will be their OWN FAULTS, if the feveral ftates fuffer the *federal sovereignty* to interfere in things of their refpective jurifdictions. An inftance of fuch interference with regard to *any fingle ftate,* will be a dangerous *precedent as to all,* and therefore will be guarded againft *by all,* as the truftees or fervants of the feveral ftates will not dare, if they retain their fenfes, fo to violate the *independent fovereignty* of their refpective ftates, THAT JUSTLY DARLING OBJECT of *American* affections, to which they are refponfible, befides being endeared by all the charities of life.

The common fenfe of mankind agrees to the devolutions of individual wills *in fociety ;* and if it has not been as univerfally affented to *in confederation,* the reafons are evident, and worthy of being retained in remembrance by *Americans.* They were want of opportunities, or the lofs of them, through defects of knowledge and virtue. The principle however has been fufficiently vindicated in imperfect combinations, as their profperity has generally been commenfurate to its operation.

How beautifully and forcibly does the infpired Apoftle *Paul,* argue upon a fublimer fubject, with a train of reafoning ftrictly applicable to the prefent ? His words are—" If the foot fhall fay, becaufe I am not the hand, I am not of the body ; is it therofore not of the body ? and if the ear fhall fay, becaufe I am

not the eye, I am not of the body; is it therefore not of the body?" As plainly inferring,
as could be done in that allegorical manner,
the strongest censure of such partial discontents
and dissentions, especially, as his meaning is
enforced by his description of the *benefits* of
union in these expressions—" But, *now* they are
many members, yet but *one body*: and the eye
CANNOT say to the hand, *I have no need of thee;*
nor again, the head to the feet, *I have no need
of you.*"

When the commons of *Rome* upon a rupture
with the Senate, seceded in arms at the *Mons
sacer, Menenius Agrippa* used the like allusion
to the human body, in his famous apologue of
a quarrel among some of the members. The
unpolished but honest-hearted *Romans* of that
day, understood him, and were appeased.

Another comparison has been made by the
learned, between a natural and a political *body;*
and no wonder indeed, when the title of the
latter was borrowed from the resemblance. It
has therefore been justly observed, that if a
mortification takes place in *one or some* of the
limbs, and *the rest* of the body is found, reme-
dies may be applied, and not only the contagion prevented from spreading, but the diseased
part or parts *saved by the connection* with the
body, and restored to former usefulness.—
When general putrefaction prevails, death is
to be expected. History sacred and profane
tells us, that, CORRUPTION OF MANNERS
SINKS NATIONS INTO SLAVERY.

FABIUS.

LETTER IV.

ANOTHER queſtion remains. *How are the contributed rights to be managed?* The reſolution has been in great meaſure anticipated, by what has been ſaid concerning the ſyſtem propoſed. Some few reflections may perhaps finiſh it.

If it be conſidered ſeparately, a CONSTITUTION is the ORGANIZATION of *the contributed rights* in ſociety. GOVERNMENT is the EXERCISE of them. It is intended for the benefit of *the governed;* of courſe can have no juſt powers but what conduce to *that end:* and the awfulneſs of the *truſt* is demonſtrated in this—that it is founded on the nature of man, that is, on the will of his MAKER, and is *therefore* ſacred. It is then an offence againſt heaven, to violate that *truſt.**

* " *We have now traced Man from a natural individual to a member of ſociety*————*Civil power, properly conſidered as ſuch is made up of the* AGGREGATE *of that claſs of the* natural *rights, which become defective in the individual in point of* power, *and* ANSWERS NOT HIS PURPOSE ; *but when* collected *into a focus, becomes competent to the purpoſe of every one.*————*Let us now apply thoſe principles to* government.————
· Individuals themſelves, *each in his ownperſonal and ſovereign right,* entered into a compact with each other, *to produce* a government ; *and this is the only mode in which governments have a*

If the organization of a conftitution be defective, it may be amended.

A good conftitution promotes, but not always produces a good adminiftration.

The government muft never be lodged in *a single body*. From fuch an one, *with an unlucky compofition* of its parts, rafh, partial, illegal, and when intoxicated with fuccefs, even cruel, infolent and contemptible edicts, may at times be expected. By *thefe*, if other mifchiefs do not follow, *the national dignity may be impaired*.

---

right to arife, and the only principle on which they have a right to exift.

A CONSTITUTION *is not a thing in name only, but in fact—It has not an ideal but a real exiftence, and wherever it cannot be produced in a vifible form, there is none. A* CONSTITUTION *is a thing* antecedent *to a* GOVERNMENT; *and a government is only* the *creature of a conftitution.— A conftitution of a country is not the act of its government, but of the people conftituting a government. It is the body of elements to which you can refer, and quote article by article; and which contains the principles on which the government fhall be eftablifhed, the manner in which it fhall be organized, the powers it fhall have, the mode of election, the duration of parliaments, or by what other name fuch bodies may be called, the powers which the executive part of the government fhall have; and, in fine, every thing that relates to the complete* ORGANIZATION *of a civil government, and the principles on which it fhall act, and by which it fhall be bound.* Rights of Man, p. 35, 36.

Several inconveniences might attend a divifion of the government into *two* bodies, that
probably would be avoided in another arrangement.

The judgment of *the moſt enlightened* among
mankind, confirmed by *multiplied experiments,*
points out the propriety of government being
committed to ſuch a number of great departments, as can be introduced *without confuſion,*
diſtinct in office, and yet connected in operation.
It ſeems to be agreed, that *three* or *four* of theſe
departments are a competent number.

" *What is a* conſtitution ? *it is the* form of
government, *delineated by the mighty hand of the*
people, in which certain firſt principles *or funda-*
mental laws are eſtabliſhed. The conſtitution is
certain and fixed ; it contains the permanent will of
the people, and is the ſupreme law of the land ; it
is paramount to the power of the legiſlature, and
can be revoked or altered only by the authority that
made it.——What are legiſlatures ? *creatures of the*
conſtitution, *they owe their* exiſtence *to the* conſtitution——*they derive their* powers *from the* conſtitution——*It is their* commiſſion, *and therefore*
all their acts muſt be conformable to it, or elſe void.
The CONSTITUTION *is the work or* will *of the*
PEOPLE THEMSELVES, *in their original, ſove-*
reign, and unlimited capacity. Law is the work
or will of the legiſlature in their derivative capacity."

Judge Patterſon's *charge to the Jury in the* Wi-
oming *caſe of* Vanhorne's *leſſee againſt* Dorrance;
tried at the circuit-court for the United States,
held at Philadelphia, April term, 1795.

Such a repartition appears well calculated to exprefs the fenfe of *the people*, and to encreafe the fafety and repofe of *the governed*, which, with the advancement of their happinefs in other refpects, are the objects of government; as thereby there will be more obftructions interpofed; againft errors, feuds, and frauds, in the adminiftration, and the *extraordinary interference of the people need be lefs frequent.* Thus, wars, tumults, and uneafineffes, are avoided. The departments fo conftituted, may *therefore* be faid to be *balanced.*

But, notwithftanding, it muft be granted, that a bad adminiftration may take place.— What is then to be done? The anfwer is inftantly found—Let the *Fafces* be lowered before —the *fupreme fovereignty* of the people. IT IS THEIR DUTY TO WATCH, AND THEIR RIGHT TO TAKE CARE, THAT THE CONSTITUTION BE PRESERVED; or in the *Roman* phrafe on perilous occafions—TO PROVIDE, THAT THE REPUBLIC RECEIVE NO DAMAGE.

Political bodies are *properly* faid to be *balanced*, with refpect to this PRIMARY ORIGINATION and ULTIMATE DESTINATION, not to any intrinfic or conftitutional properties.* It

* *Conftitutional properties are only, as has been obferved at the beginning of this letter, parts in the organization of the contributed rights. As long as thofe parts preferve the orders affigned to them refpectively by the conftitution, they may fo far be faid to be balanced: but, when one part, without being fufficiently checked by the reft, abufes its power to*

..is the POWER from which they PROCEED, and which they SERVE, that TRULY AND OF RIGHT BALANCES them. †

But, as a good conſtitution not always produces a good adminiſtration, a defective one not always excludes it. Thus, in governments very different from thoſe of *United America*, general manners and cuſtoms, improvement in knowledge, and the education and diſpoſition of princes, not unfrequently ſoften the features,

---

the manifeſt danger of public happineſs, or when the ſeveral parts abuſe their reſpective powers ſo as to involve the commonwealth in the like peril, THE PEOPLE *muſt reſtore things to that order, from which their functionaries have departed. If* THE PEOPLE *ſuffer this living principle of* watchfulneſs and controul *to be extinguiſhed among them, they will aſſuredly not long afterwards experience that of their " temple," " there ſhall not be left one ſtone upon another, that ſhall not be thrown down."*

† *When the* CONTROULING POWER *is in a* conſtitution, *it has the* NATION *for its ſupport, and the* NATURAL *and the political controuling powers are together. The laws which are enacted by governments, controul men only as individuals, but the* NATION, *thro' its conſtitution controuls* THE WHOLE GOVERNMENT, *and has a* NATURAL ABILITY *to do ſo. The* FINAL CONTROULING *power, therefore, and the* ORIGINAL CONSTITUTING *power,* ARE ONE AND THE SAME POWER.

Rights of Man, 1792. *part* 2d, *b.* 4, *p.* 42.

and qualify the defects. Jewels of value are substituted, in the place of the rare and genuine orient of highest price and brightest lustre : and though the sovereigns *cannot* even in their ministers, be brought to account by the governed, yet there are instances of their conduct indicating a veneration for the rights of the people, and an internal conviction of the guilt that attends their violation. Some of them appear to be *fathers of their countries.* Revered princes ! *Friends of mankind !* May peace be in their lives—and in their deaths—Hope.

By this superior will of the people, is meant a reasonable, not a distracted will. When frenzy seizes the mass, it would be equal madness to think of their happiness, that is, of their freedom. They will infallibly have a *Philip* or a *Cæsar*, to bleed them into soberness of mind. At present we are cool ; and let us attend to our business.

Our government under the proposed confederation, will be guarded by a repetition of the strongest cautions against excesses. In the *senate* the *sovereignties* of the several states will be *equally* represented ; in *the house of representatives*, the *people* of the whole union will be *equally represented* ; and, in the *president*, and the federal independent *judges*, so much concerned in the execution of the laws, and in the determination of their constitutionality, the *sovereignties* of the several states and *the people* of the whole union, may be considered as *conjointly* represented.

Where was there ever and where is there now upon the face of the earth, a government so diversified and attempered? If a work formed with so much deliberation, so respectful and affectionate an attention to the interests, feelings, and sentiments of all *United America*, will not satisfy, what would satisfy all *United America?*

It seems highly probable, that those who would reject this labour of public love, would also have rejected the Heaven-taught institution of TRIAL BY JURY, had they been consulted upon its establishment. Would they not have cried out, that there never was framed so detestable, so paltry, and so tyrannical a device for extinguishing freedom, and throwing unbounded domination into the hands of the king and barons, under a contemptible pretence of preserving it? "What! Can *freedom* be preserved by *imprisoning* its *guardians?* Can *freedom* be preserved, by keeping *twelve* men *closely confined* without *meat, drink, fire*, or *candle*, until they *unanimously agree*, and this to be innumerably repeated? Can *freedom* be preserved, by thus delivering up *a number of freemen* to a *monarch* and an *aristocracy*, fortified by *dependant* and *obedient* judges and officers, to be shut up, *until under duress they speak as they are ordered?* Why cannot the twelve jurors *separate,** after hearing the evidence, return to their *respective homes*, and there *take time,** and *think* of the matter *at their ease?** Is there not *a variety of*

---

* *See late publications against the Federal Constitution.*

ways, in which caufes have been, and can be tried, without this TREMENDOUS, UNPRECEDENTED INQUISITION? Why then is it infifted on; but becaufe the fabricators of it *know* that it *will*, and *intend* that it *fhall* reduce the people to flavery? Away with it—Freemen will never be enthralled by fo infolent, fo execrable, fo pitiful a contrivance."

Happily for us our anceftors thought otherwife. They were not fo over-nice and curious, as to refufe bleffings, becaufe, they might poffibly be abufed.

They perceived, that the *ufes* included were great and manifeft. Perhaps they did not forefee, that from this acorn, as it were, of their planting, would be produced a perpetual vegetation of political energies, that " would fecure the juft liberties of the nation for a long fucceffion of ages,* and elevate it to the diftinguifhed rank it has for feveral centuries held. As to *abufes*, they trufted to their own fpirit for preventing or correcting them: And worthy is it of deep confideration by every friend of freedom, that *abufes* that feem to be but " *trifles*," † may be attended by fatal confequences. What can be " *trifling*," that diminifhes or detracts from the only defence, that ever was found againft " *open attacks* and *fecret machinations?* ‡ This eftablifhment originates from a knowledge of human nature. With a fuperior force, wifdom, and benevolence uni-

* *Blackftone*, III. 379. † *Idem*, IV. 350.
‡ *Idem*, III. 381.

F

ted, it rives the difficulties concerning administration of justice, that have distressed, or destroyed the rest of mankind. It reconciles contradictions—*vastness of power*, with *safety of private station*. It is *ever new*, and *always the same*.

Trial by jury and the dependance of taxation upon representation, those corner stones of liberty, were not obtained by *a bill of rights*, or any other records, and have not been and cannot be preserved by them. They and all other rights must be preserved, by SOUNDNESS OF SENSE and HONESTY OF HEART. Compared with *these*, what are a bill of rights, or any characters drawn upon *paper* or *parchment*, those frail remembrancers? Do we want to be reminded, that the sun enlightens, warms, invigorates, and cheers? or how horrid it would be, to have his blessed beams intercepted, by our being thrust into mines or dungeons? Liberty is the sun of society. Rights are the beams.*

---

* *Instead of referring to musty* records *and mouldy* parchments *to prove that the rights of the living are lost,* " *renounced, and abdicated for ever*," *by those who are now no more.*——M. *de la* Fayette, *in his address to the national assembly, applies to the living world, and says*—" *Call to mind the sentiments which nature has engraved in the heart of every citizen, and which take a new face when they are solemnly* recognized by all. *For a nation to love* liberty, *it is sufficient that she knows it; and to be free, it is sufficient that she wills it.*"

Rights of Man, *p.* 11.

"It is the duty which every man owes to his country, his friends, his posterity, and himself, to maintain to the utmost of his power this valuable palladium in all its rights ; to restore it to its ancient dignity, if at all impaired by the different value of property, or otherwife deviated from its firft inftitution ; to *amend* it, wherever it is *defective ;* * and above all to guard with the moft jealous circumfpection againft the new and arbitrary methods of trial, which, under a variety of plaufible pretences, may in time imperceptibly undermine this beft prefervative of liberty."† Trial by Jury is our *birth-right ;* and tempted to his own ruin, by fome feducing fpirit, muft be the man, who in oppofition to the genius of *United America,* fhall dare to attempt its fubverfion.

In the propofed confederation, it is preferved inviolable in criminal cafes, and cannot be altered in other refpects, but when *United America* demands it.

There feems to be a difpofition in men to find fault, no difficult matter, rather than to act as they ought. The works of creation itfelf have been objected to : and one learned prince declared, that if *he* had been confulted, they would have been improved. With what book has fo much fault been found, as with the *Bible?* Perhaps, principally, becaufe it *fo clearly and ftrongly enjoins men* TO DO RIGHT. How many, how plaufible objections have been

***

* *See an enumeration of* defects *in trials by jury,* Blackftone, III. 381. † *Idem,* IV. 350.

made againſt it, with how much ardor, with how much pains? Yet, the book has done more good than all the books in the world; would do much more, if duly regarded; and might lead the objectors againſt it to happineſs, if they would value it as they ſhould.

When *objections* are made to a ſyſtem of high import, ſhould they not be weighed againſt the *benefits?* Are *theſe* great, poſitive, immediate? Is there a chance of endangering them by rejection or delay? MAY THEY NOT BE ATTAINED WITHOUT ADMITTING THE OBJECTIONS AT PRESENT, ſuppoſing the objections to be well founded? If the objections are well founded, may they not be hereafter admitted, without danger, diſguſt, or inconvenience? Is the ſyſtem ſo formed, that they may be thus admitted? May they not be of leſs efficacy, than they are thought to be by their authors? are they not deſigned to hinder evils, which are generally deemed to be ſufficiently provided againſt? May not the admiſſion of them prevent benefits, that might otherwiſe be obtained? In political affairs, is it not more ſafe and advantageous, for *all* to agree in meaſures that may not be beſt, than to quarrel *among themſelves*, what are beſt?

When queſtions of this kind with regard to the plan propoſed, are *calmly conſidered*, it ſeems reaſonable to hope, that every faithful citizen of *United America*, will make up his mind, with much ſatisfaction to himſelf, and advantage to his country.

FABIUS.

LETTER V.

IT has been confidered, *what are the rights to be contributed*, and *how they are to be managed*; and it has been faid, that republican tranquility and profperity have commonly been promoted, in proportion to the ftrength of government for protecting *the worthy* againft *the licentious.*

The protection herein mentioned, refers to cafes *between* citizens and citizens, or ftates and ftates: But there is alfo a protection to be afforded to *all* the citizens, or ftates, againft foreigners. It has been afferted, that *this* protection never can be afforded, but under an appropriation, collection, and application, of the general force, by the will of the whole combination. This protection is in a degree dependant on the former, as it may be weakened by internal difcords and efpecially where the worft party prevails. Hence it is evident, that fuch eftablifhments as tend moft to protect *the worthy* againft *the licentious*, tend moft to protect *all* againft foreigners. This pofition is found to be verified by indifputable facts, from which it appears, that when nations have been, as it were, *condemned* for their *crimes*, unlefs they firft became *fuicides*, foreigners have acted as *executioners.*

This is not all. As government is intended for the happinefs of the people, the protection of the worthy againft thofe of contrary characters, is calculated to promote the end of legitimate government, that is, *the general welfare;*

for THE GOVERNMENT WILL PARTAKE OF THE QUALITIES OF THOSE WHOSE AUTHORITY IS PREVALENT. If it be afked, who are *the worthy*, we may be informed by a heathen poet—

"Vir *bonus* eft quis ?
"Qui *confulta patrum*, qui *leges juraque* fervat."*

The beft foundations of this protection, that can be laid by men, are a conftitution and government fecured, as well as can be, from the undue influence of *paffions* either in *the people* or *their fervants*. Then in a conteft between citizens and citizens, or ftates and ftates, the ftandard of *laws* may be difplayed, explained and ftrengthened by the well-remembered fentiments and examples of our fore-fathers, which will give it a fanctity far fuperior to that of their eagles fo venerated by the former mafters of the world. This circumftance will carry powerful aids to the true friends of their country, and unlefs counteracted by the follies of *Pharfalia*, or the accidents of *Philippi*, may fecure the bleffings of freedom to fucceeding ages.

It has been contended, that the plan propofed to us, adequately fecures us againft the influence of *paffions* in the federal fervants. Whether it as adequately fecures us againft the influence of *paffions* in the people, or in particular ftates, *time will determine*, and MAY THE DETERMINATION BE PROPITIOUS.

---

* *He who reveres the conftitution, liberties and laws of his country.*————

Let us now confider the tragical play of the paffions in fimilar cafes; or, in other words, the confequences of their irregularities. Duly governed, they produce happinefs.

Here the reader, is refpectfully requefted, to affift the intentions of the writer, by keeping in mind, the ideas of a fingle republic with *one* democratic branch in its government, and of a confederation of republics with *one* or *feveral* democratic branches in the government of the confederation, or in the government of its parts, fo that as he proceeds, a comparifon may eafily run along, between any of thefe and the pro-pofed plan.

Hiftory is entertaining and inftructive; but, if admired chiefly for amufement, it may yield little profit. If read for improvement, it is apprehended, a flight attention only will be paid to the vaft variety of particular incidents, un-lefs they be fuch as may meliorate the heart. A knowledge of the diftinguifhing features of nations, the principles of their governments, the advantages and difadvantages of their fitua-tions, the methods employed to avail them-felves of the firft, and to alleviate the laft, their manners, cuftoms, and inftitutions, the fources of events, their progreffes, and determining caufes, may be eminently ufeful, tho' obfcu-rity may reft upon a multitude of attending circumftances. Thus, one nation may become prudent and happy, not only by the wifdom and fuccefs, but even by the errors and misfor-tunes of another.

In *Carthage* and *Rome*, there was a very numerous *senate*, ſtrengthened by prodigious attachments, and in a great degree independent of the people. In *Athens*, there was a ſenate ſtrongly ſupported by the powerful court of *Areopagus*. In each of theſe republics, their affairs at length became convulſed, and their liberty was ſubverted. What cauſe produced theſe effects? Encroachments of the *senate* upon the authority of the people? No! but directly the reverſe, according to the unanimous voice of hiſtorians; that is, encroachments of the *people* upon the authority of the ſenate. The *people* of theſe republics abſolutely LABOURED for their own deſtruction; and never thought themſelves *ſo free*, as when they were promoting their own ſubjugation. Though, even after theſe encroachments had been made, and ruin was ſpreading around, yet, *the remnants of ſenatorial authority* delayed the final cataſtrophe.*

---

* *The great* Bacon, *in enumerating the art by which* Cæſar *enſlaved his country, ſays—"His* firſt artifice *was to break the ſtrength of the* SENATE, *for while that remained ſafe, there was no opening for any perſon to immoderate or extraordinary power,——"Nam* initio *ſibi erant frangendæ* ſenatus opes et autoritas qua ſalva nemini ad, immodica et extra ordinaria imperia aditus erat." Boſſuet, *biſhop of* Meaux, *takes notice in his univerſal hiſtory, that the infamous* Herod, *to engroſs authority, attacked the* Sanhedrim, *which was in a manner the ſenate, where the ſupreme juriſdiction was exerciſed."*

In more modern times, the *Florentines* exhibited a memorable example. They were divided into violent parties; and the prevailing one vested exorbitant powers in the house of *Medici*, then poffeffed, as it was judged, of more money, than any crowned head in *Europe*. Though that houfe engaged and perfevered in the attempt, yet the people were never defpoiled of their liberty, until they were overwhelmed by the armies of foreign princes, to whofe enterprizes their fituation expofed them.

Republics of later date and various form have appeared. Their inftitutions confift of old errors tiffued with hafty inventions, fomewhat excufable, as the wills of the *Romans*, made with arms in their hands. *Some* of them were *condenfed* *, by dangers. They are ftill compreffed by them into a fort of union. Their well-known tranfactions witnefs, that *their connection is not enough compact and arranged*. They have all fuffered, or *are fuffering* through *that defect*. Their exiftence feems to depend more upon others, than upon themfelves. There might be an impropriety in faying more, confidering the peculiarity of their circumftances *at this time*.

---

* " *If we confider what the principles are that firft* condenfe *man into fociety, and what the motive is that regulates their mutual intercourfe afterwards, we fhall find, by the time we arrive at what is called government, that nearly the whole of the bufinefs is performed by the natural operation of the parts upon each other.*" Rights of Man.

The wretched miſtake of the great men who were leaders in the long parliament of *England*, in attempting, by not filling up vacancies, to extend their power over a brave and ſenſible people, accuſtomed to POPULAR REPRESEN-TATION, and their downfal, when their victories and puiſſance by ſea and land had thrown all *Europe* into aſtoniſhment and awe, ſhew, how difficult it is for rulers to uſurp over a people who are not wanting to themſelves.

Let the fortunes of *confederated* republics be now conſidered.

"*The Amphictionic council*," or "general court of *Greece*," claims the firſt regard. Its authority was very great: But, the parts were not ſufficiently combined, to guard againſt the ambitious, avaricious, and ſelfiſh projects of ſome of them; or, if they had the power, they dared not to employ it, as the turbulent ſtates were very ſturdy, and made a ſort of partial confederacies. *

---

* *When* Xerxes *invaded* Greece *with the largeſt hoſt and the greateſt fleet that ever were collected, events occurred, which being preſerved in hiſtory, convey to us a very affecting and inſtructive information.*

While the danger was at ſome diſtance, the ſtates of Greece *looked to remote friends for aſſiſtance. Diſappointed in theſe ſpeculations, tho' the vaſt armaments of their enemies were conſtantly rolling towards them, ſtill there was no firmneſs in their union, no vigor in their reſolutions.*

" *The Achæan league*" feems to be the next
in dignity. It was at firſt, fmall, confiſting of
few ſtates : afterwards, very extenſive, conſiſt-
ing of many. In their diet or Congreſs, they
enacted laws, diſpoſed of vacant employments,
declared war, made peace, entered into alliances, compelled every ſtate of the union to

---

The Perfian *army paſſed the* Hellefpont, *and
directed its march weſtward. It was then decided,
that* Theſſaly *was the frontier to be firſt attacked.*

The Theſſalians, *than whom no people had been
more forward in the common cauſe haſtened a remonſtrance to* Corinth, *urging that unleſs they were
immediately and powerfully ſupported, neceſſity would
oblige them to make terms with the invaders.*

*This reaſonable remonſtrance rouſed the ſluggiſh
and heſitating councils of the confederacy. A body of
foot was diſpatched who ſoon occupied the valley of*
Tempe, *the only paſs from* Lower Macedonia
into Theſſaly.

*In a few days, theſe troops being informed that
there was another paſs from* Upper Macedonia,
returned to the Corinthian *iſthmus.*

The Theſſalians *thus deſerted made their ſub-
miſſion.*

" *This retreat from* Tempe *appears to have been
a precipitate meaſure, rendered neceſſary by nothing
ſo much as by* THE WANT OF SOME POWERS *of
government extending over the ſeveral ſtates which
compoſed the confederacy.*"

Mitford's *Hiſtory of* Greece.
*With diminiſhed forces, the defence of the confe-
derates was now to be contracted. But in the con-*

G 2

obey its ordinances, and managed other affairs.
Not only their laws, but their magistrates,
council, judges, money, weights and measures,
were the same. So uniform were they, that
all seemed to be but one state. Their chief
officer called *Strategos*, was chosen in the Congress by a majority of votes. He presided in

---

duct even of this business daily becoming more urgent,
we find them labouring under the defects of their
confederation.

Destitute of any sufficient power *extending over
the whole, no* part *could confide in the protection of*
the whole, *while the naval superiority of their
enemy put it in his choice, where, when, and how
to make his attacks; and therefore each republic
seems to have been anxious to reserve* its own
strength for future contingencies.

*Their generous hearts all beat at the call of
freedom; but their efforts were embarrassed and en-
feebled by* the vices of their political constitution,
*to their prodigious detriment, and almost to their
total destruction.* For these *vices, the ardor of
heroism united with love of country could not com-
pensate. These very vices therefore, may truly be
said to have wasted the blood of patriots, and to
have betrayed their country into the severest calamities.*

If we *shall hereafter by* experience *discover any
vices in* our *constitution, let us* HASTEN *with prudence and a fraternal affection for each other, to
correct them.* We are all *embarked in the same
vessel, and equally concerned in repairing any defects.*

the Congrefs, commanded the forces, and was vefted with great powers, efpecially in time of war: but was liable to be called to an account by the Congrefs, and punifhed, if convicted of mifbehaviour.

These ftates had been oppreffed by the kings of *Macedon*, and infulted by tyrants. "From their incorporation," fays *Polybius*, " may be dated the birth of that greatnefs, that by a con-ftant augmentation, at length arrived to a mar-vellous height of profperity. 'The fame of their *wife laws* and *mild government* reached the *Greek* colonies in *Italy*, where the *Crotoniates*, the *Sybarites*, and the *Cauloniates*, agreed to a-dopt them, and to govern their ftates confor-mably."

Did the delegates to *the Amphictionic council*, or to *the Congrefs of the Achæan league*, deftroy the liberty of their country, by eftablifhing a monarchy or an ariftocracy among themfelves? Quite the contrary. WHILE THE SEVERAL STATES CONTINUED FAITHFUL TO THE UNION, THEY PROSPERED. Their affairs were fhattered by diffentions, emulations, and civil wars, artfully and diligently fomented by princes who thought it their intereft; and in the cafe of *the Achæan league*, partly, by the fol-ly and wickednefs of *Greeks* not of the league, particularly the *Ætolians*, who repined at the glories, that conftantly attended the banner of freedom, fupported by virtue, and conducted by prudence. *Thus weakened*, they all funk toge-ther, the envied and the envying, under the domination, firft of *Macedon*, and then of *Rome*.

Let any man of common fenfe perufe the gloomy but inftructive pages of their mournful ftory, and he will be convinced, that if any nation could fuccefsfully have refifted thofe conquerors of the world, the illuftrious deed had been atchieved by *Greece*, that cradle of republics; if the feveral ftates had been cemented by fome fuch league as the *Achæan*, and had *honeftly fulfilled its obligations*.

It is not pretended, that *the Achæan league* was perfect, or that there were not monarchical and ariftocratical factions among the people of it. Every conceffion of that fort, that can be afked, fhall be made. It had many defects; every one of which, however, has been avoided in the plan propofed to us.

With all its defects, with all its diforders, yet fuch was the life and vigor communicated through *the whole*, by the *popular reprefentation* of each part, and by the *clofe combination* of all, that the true fpirit of republicanifm PREDOMINATED, and thereby advanced the happinefs and glory of the people to fo pre-eminent a ftate, that OUR ideas upon the pleafing theme cannot be too elevated. Here is the proof of this affertion. When the *Romans* had laid *Carthage* in afhes; had reduced the kingdom of *Macedon* to a province; had conquered *Antiochus* the great, and got the better of all their enemies in the *Eaft*; thefe *Romans*, mafters of fo much of the then known world, determined to humble the *Achæan league*, becaufe as hiftory exprefsly informs us, " *their great power began to raife no fmall jealoufy at Rome*." Polybius.

What a vaſt weight of argument do theſe facts and circumſtances add to the maintenance of the principle contended for by the writer of this addreſs ?

F A B I U S.

LETTER VI.

SOME of our fellow-citizens have ventured to predict the future fate of *United America*, if the fyftem propofed to us, fhall be adopted.

Though, every branch of the conftitution and government is to be popular, and guarded by the ftrongeft provifions, that until this day have occurred to mankind, yet the fyftem will end, they fay, in the oppreffions of *a monarchy or ariftocracy* by the federal fervants or fome of them.

Such a conclufion feems not in any manner fuited to the premifes. It ftartles, yet, not fo much from its novelty, as from the refpectability of the characters by which it is drawn.

We muft not be too much influenced by our efteem for thofe characters : But, fhould recollect, that when the fancy is warmed, and the judgment inclined, by the proximity or preffure of particular objects, very extraordinary declarations are not unfrequently made. Such are the frailties of our nature, that genius and integrity fometimes afford no protection againft them.

Probably, there never was, and never will be, fuch an inftance of dreadful denunciation, concerning the fate of a country, as was publifhed while the union was in agitation between *England* and *Scotland*. The *Englifh* were for a joint legiflature, many of the *Scots* for feparate legiflatures, and urged, that they fhould be in a manner fwallowed up and loft in the other, as then *they* would not poffefs *one eleventh* part in it.

Upon that occafion lord *Eelhaven*, one of the moft diftinguifhed orators of the age, made in the *Scottifh* parliament a famous fpeech, of which the following extract is part:

" My lord Chancellor,

" When I confider this affair of an *union* between the two nations, as it is exprefled in the feveral articles thereof, and now the fubject of our deliberation at this time, I find my mind crowded with a variety of *very melancholy thoughts*, and I think it my duty to difburthen myfelf of fome of them, by laying them before and expofing them to the ferious confideration of this honourable houfe.

" I think, I SEE A FREE AND INDEPENDENT KINGDOM delivering up *that*, which all the world hath been fighting for fince the days of *Nimrod*; yea, *that*, for which moft of all the empires, kingdoms, ftates, principalities and dukedoms of *Europe*, are at this very time engaged in the moft bloody and cruel wars that ever were; *to wit*, A POWER TO MANAGE THEIR OWN AFFAIRS BY THEMSELVES, WITHOUT THE ASSISTANCE AND COUNCIL OF ANY OTHER.

" I think, I fee A NATIONAL CHURCH, founded upon a rock, fecured by *a claim of right*, hedged and fenced about by the ftricteft and pointedeft legal fanctions that fovereignty could contrive, voluntarily defcending into a plain, upon an equal level with *Jews, Papifts, Soci-*

H

nians, *Arminians*, *Anabaptifts*, and other Secta-
ries, &c.

" I think, I fee THE NOBLE AND HONOR-
ABLE PEERAGE OF SCOTLAND, whofe vali-
ant predeceffors led armies againft their enemies
upon their own proper charges and expences,
now divefted of their followers and vaffalages,
and put upon fuch an equal foot with their
vaffals, that I think, I fee a petty *Englifh* EX-
CISEMAN receive more homage and refpect,
than what was paid formerly to their *quondam*
Mackallamors.

" I think, I fee THE PRESENT PEERS OF
SCOTLAND, whofe noble anceflors conquered
provinces, over-run countries, reduced and fub-
jected towns and fortified places, exacted tri-
bute through the greateft part of *England*, now
walking in THE COURT OF REQUESTS, like
fo many *Englifh* Attornies, laying afide their
walking fwords when in company with the
Englifh Peers, left their felf-defence fhould be
found murder.

" I think, I fee THE HONORABLE ESTATE
OF BARONS, the bold afferters of the nation's
rights and liberties in the worft of times, now
fetting A WATCH UPON THEIR LIPS and A
GUARD UPON THEIR TONGUES, left they be
found guilty of SCANDALUM MAGNATUM.

" I think, I fee THE ROYAL STATE OF BO-
ROUGHS, walking their DESOLATE STREETS,
hanging down their heads UNDER DISAPPOINT-
MENTS; worm'd out of ALL THE BRANCHES
OF THEIR OLD TRADE, uncertain WHAT
HAND TO TURN TO, neceffitated to become

apprentices to their unkind neighbours, and yet after all finding their TRADE SO FORTIFIED BY COMPANIES and fecured by prefcriptions, that they defpair of any fuccefs therein.

" I think, I fee OUR LEARNED JUDGES laying afide *their practiques & decifions*, ftudying the common law of *England*, gravelled with *certioraries, nifi priufes, writs of error, ejectiones firmæ, injunctions, demurrers*, &c. and frighted with APPEALS and AVOCATIONS, becaufe of THE NEW REGULATIONS, and RECTIFICATIONS they meet with.

" I think, I fee THE VALIANT AND GALLANT SOLDIERY, either fent to learn the plantation trade abroad, or at home petitioning for A SMALL SUBSISTENCE, as the reward of their honourable exploits, while their old corps are broken, the common foldiers left to beg, and the youngeft *Englifh* corps kept ftanding.

" I think, I fee THE HONEST INDUSTRIOUS TRADESMAN loaded with NEW TAXES AND IMPOSITIONS, difappointed of the equivalents, drinking water in place of ale, eating his faltlefs pottage, petitioning for ENCOURAGEMENT TO HIS MANUFACTORIES, and anfwered by counter petitions.

" In fhort, I think I fee THE LABORIOUS PLOUGHMAN, with his corn fpoiling upon his hands FOR WANT OF SALE, curfing the day of his birth; dreading the expence of his burial, and uncertain whether to marry, or do worfe.

" I think, I fee the incurable difficulties of LANDING MEN, fettered under the golden chain of equivalents, their pretty daughters petitioning for want of husbands, and their sons for want of employments.

"I think, I see OUR MARINERS DELIVERING UP THEIR SHIPS to their *Dutch* partners, and what through PRESSES AND NECESSITY *earning their bread as underlings* in the *English* navy. But above all, my lord, I think, I see OUR ANTIENT MOTHER CALEDONIA, like *Cæsar*, sitting in the midst of our senate, *ruefully looking round about her*, covering herself with her royal garment, *attending the fatal blows* and breathing out her last with a———*Et tu quoque, mi fili.*

"Are not these, my lord, *very afflicting thoughts?* And yet they are the least part suggested to me *by these dishonorable articles.* Should not the considerations of these things vivify these *dry bones* of ours? Should not the *memory of our noble predecessors' valor and constancy* rouse up our drooping spirits? Are our noble predecessors, souls got so far into the *English cabbage-stalks and cauliflowers,* that we should shew the least inclination that way? Are our eyes *so blinded?* Are our ears *so deafened?* Are our hearts *so hardened?* Are our tongues *so faultered?* Are our hands *so fettered?* that in *this our day,* I say, my lord, *that in this our day, we should not mind the things that concern the very being and well being of our ancient kingdom, before the day be hid from our eyes.*

"When I consider this treaty as it hath been explained, and spoke to, before us these three weeks by past; I see the ENGLISH constitution remaining firm, the same TWO HOUSES of Parliament, the fame TAXES, the fame CUSTOMS, the fame EXCISES, the fame TRADING COMPANIES, the fame municipal laws and courts of judicature; and ALL OURS EITHER SUBJECT TO REGULATIONS OR ANNIHILATIONS, only *we* are to have THE HONOR to pay THEIR OLD DEBTS, and to have *fome few perfons prefent for witneffes* to the validity of the deed, when they are pleafed to contract more."*

Let any candid *American* deliberately compare that tranfaction with the prefent, and laying his hand upon his heart, folemnly anfwer this queftion to himfelf—Whether, he does not verily believe the eloquent Peer before mentioned, had ten-fold more caufe to apprehend evils from fuch an unequal match between the two kingdoms, than any citizen of thefe ftates has to apprehend them from the fyftem propofed? Indeed not only that Peer, but other perfons of diftinction, and large numbers of the people of *Scotland* were filled with the utmoft averfion to the union; and if the greateft diligence and prudence had not been employed by its friends in removing mifapprehenfions and refuting mifreprefentations, and by the then fubfifting government for preferving the public peace, there would certainly have been a rebellion.

Yet, WHAT WERE THE CONSEQUENCES to *Scotland* of that DREADED union with *England*? The cultivation of her virtues, and the correction of her errors—The emancipation of one

* *See objections againſt the Federal conſtitution, very fimilar to thofe made in Scotland.*

clafs of her citizens from the yoke of their fu-
periors—A relief of other claffes from the injuries and infults of the great—Improvements in
agriculture, fcience, arts, trade, and manufac-
tures—The profits of induftry and ingenuity
enjoyed under the protection of laws—peace
and fecurity at home, and encreafe of refpectability abroad. Her *Church* is ftill *eminent*—Her
laws and *courts of judicature* are fafe—Her *bo-
roughs* grown into cities—Her *mariners* and *foldiery* poffeffing *a larger fubfiftence*, than fhe could
have afforded them, and her *tradefmen*, *plough-
men*, *landed men*, and her people of every rank,
in a more flourifhing condition, not only than
they ever were, but in a more flourifhing condition, than the cleareft underftanding could, at
the time, have thought it poffible for them to
attain in *fo fhort a period*, or even in many ages.
England participated in the bleffings. The *ftock*
of their union, or *ingraftment*, as perhaps it
may be called, being ftrong, and capable of
drawing better nutriment and in greater abundance, than they could ever have done apart,

" Ere long, to Heaven the foaring branches fhoot,

" And wonder at their *height*, and *more than native fruit*."

FABIUS.

LETTER VII.

THUS happily miftaken was the ingenious, learned, and patriotic lord *Belhaven*, in his prediction concerning the fate of his country; and thus happily miftaken, it is hoped, fome of our fellow-citizens will be, in their prediction concerning the fate of their country.

Had they taken larger fcope, and affumed in their propofition the viciffitude of human affairs, and the paffions that fo often confound them, their prediction might have been a tolerably good guefs. Amidft the mutabilities of terreftrial things, the liberty of *United America* may be deftroyed. As to that point, it is our duty, humbly, conftantly, fervently, to implore the protection of our moft gracious maker, " who doth not afflict willingly nor grieve the children of men," and inceffantly to ftrive, as we are commanded, to recommend ourfelves to that protection, by " doing his will," diligently exercifing our reafon in fulfilling the purpofes for which that and our exiftence were given to us.

How the liberty of this country is to be deftroyed, is another queftion. Here, the gentlemen affign a caufe, in no manner proportioned, as it is apprehended, to the effect.

The uniform tenor of hiftory is againft them. That holds up the LICENTIOUSNESS of the people, and TURBULENT TEMPER of fome of the ftates, as THE ONLY CAUSES to be dreaded, not the confpiracies of *federal officers*. Therefore, it is highly probable, that, if our liberty is ever subverted, it will be by one of the two causes first mentioned. Our tragedy will then have the same acts, with those of the nations that have gone before us ; and we shall add one more example to the number already too great, of people that would not take warning, not, " know the things which belong to their peace." But, we ought not to pass such a sentence against our country, and the interests of freedom : Though, no sentence whatever can be equal to the atrocity of our guilt, if through enormity of *obstinacy* or *baseness*, we betray the cause of our posterity and of mankind, by providence committed to our parental and fraternal care. There is reason to believe, that the calamities of nations are the punishments of their sins.

As to the first mentioned cause, it seems unnecessary to say any more upon it.

As to the second, we find, that the misbehaviour of the *constituent parts* acting separately, or in partial confederacies, debilitated the *Greeks* under *The Amphictionic Council*, and under *The Achæan League*. As to the former, it was not entirely an assembly of strictly democratical republics. Besides, it wanted a sufficiently *close connection* of its parts. After these observations, we may call our attention from it.

'Tis true, *The Achæan League* was disturbed by the misconduct of *some parts*, but, it is as true, that it surmounted these difficulties, and wonderfully prospered, until it was dissolved in the manner that has been described.

The glorious operations of its principles bear the cleareſt teſtimony to this diſtant age and people, that the wit of man never invented ſuch an antidote againſt monarchical and ariſtocratical projects, as a *ſtrong combination* of truly *democratical* republics. By ſtrictly or truly democratical republics, the writer means republics, in which all the principal officers, except the judicial, are from time to time choſen by the people.

The reaſon is plain. As *liberty* and *equality*, or as well termed by *Polybius*, BENIGNITY, were the foundations of their inſtitutions, and the *energy* of the government pervaded *all the parts* in things relating to the whole, it counteracted for the common welfare, the deſigns hatched by ſelfiſhneſs in ſeparate councils.

If folly or wickedneſs prevailed in any *parts*, friendly offices and ſalutary meaſures reſtored tranquility. Thus the public good was maintained. In its very formation, tyrannies and ariſtocracies ſubmitted, by conſent or compulſion. *Thus*, the *Ceraunians, Trezenians, Epidaurians, Megalopolitans, Argives, Hermionians, and Phlyayzrians* were received into the league. A happy exchange! For hiſtory informs us, that ſo true were they to their *noble* and *benevolent* principles, that, in their diet, " NO RESOLUTIONS WERE TAKEN, BUT WHAT WERE EQUALLY ADVANTAGEOUS TO THE WHOLE CONFEDERACY, AND THE INTEREST OF EACH PART SO CONSULTED, AS TO LEAVE NO ROOM FOR COMPLAINTS !"

I

How degrading would be the thought to a citizen of *United America*, that the people of thefe ftates, with inftitutions beyond comparifon preferable to thofe of *The Achæan league*, and fo vaft a fuperiority in other refpects, fhould not have wifdom and virtue enough, to manage their affairs, with as much *prudence* and *affection of one for another* as thefe ancients did.

Would this be doing juftice to our country? The compofition of her temper is excellent, and feems to be acknowledged equal to that of any nation in the world. Her prudence will guard its warmth againft *two faults*, to which it may be expofed—The one, an imitation of FOREIGN FASHIONS, which from fmall things may lead to great. May her citizens afpire at *a national dignity* in every part of conduct, private as well as public. This will be influenced by the former. May SIMPLICITY be the characteriftic feature of their manners, which, inlaid with their other virtues and their forms of government, may then indeed be compared, in the Eaftern ftile, to "apples of gold in pictures of filver." Thus will they long, and may they, while their rivers run, efcape the contagion of *luxury*—that motley iffue of innocence debauched by folly, and the lineal predeceffor of tyranny, prolific of guilt and wretchednefs. The other fault, of which, *as yet*, there are no fymptoms among us, is the THIRST OF EMPIRE. This is a vice, that ever has been, and from the nature of things, ever muft be, fatal to *republican* forms of government. Our wants, are sources of happinefs : our irregular defires, of mifery. The abufe of profperity, is rebellion againft Heaven ; and fucceeds accordingly.

Do the propofitions of gentlemen who object, offer to our view, any of THE GREAT POINTS upon which, the fate, fame, or freedom of nations has turned, excepting what fome of them have faid about trial by jury; and which has been frequently and fully anfwered? Is there one of them calculated to regulate, and if needful, to CONTROUL thofe tempers and meafures of *conftituent parts* of an union, that have been fo baneful to the weal of every confederacy that has exifted ? Do not fome of them *tend to enervate the authority* evidently defigned thus to regulate and controul? Do not others of them difcover a bias in their advocates to *particular connections*, that if indulged to them, would enable perfons of lefs underftanding and virtue, to repeat the diforders, that have fo often violated public peace and honor? Taking them altogether, would they afford as ftrong a fecurity to our liberty, as the *frequent election* of the federal officers by the people, and the *repartition of power* among thofe officers, according to the propofed fyftem ?

It may be anfwered, that, they would be an additional fecurity. In reply, let the writer be permitted at prefent to refer to what has been faid.

The principal argument of gentlemen who object, involves a direct proof of the point contended for by the writer of this addrefs, and as far as it may be fuppofed to be founded, a plain confirmation of Hiftoric evidence.

They generally agree, that the great danger of a monarchy or ariftocracy among us, will arife from the federal *fenate*.

The members of this *fenate*, are to be chofen by men exercifing the fovereignty of their refpective ftates. Thefe men therefore, muft be monarchically or ariftocratically difpofed, before they will chufe federal fenators thus difpofed; and what merits particular attention, is, that thefe men muft have obtained an overbearing influence in their refpective ftates; before they could with fuch difpofition arrive at the exercife of the fovereignty in them : or elfe, the like difpofition muft be prevalent among the people of fuch ftates.

Taking the cafe either way, is not this a diforder in *parts* of the union, and ought it not to be rectified by *the reft?* Is it reafonable to expect, that the difeafe will feize *all* at the fame time ? If it is not, ought not *the found* to poffefs a right and power, by which they may prevent the infection from fpreading ? And will not THE EXTENT of our territory, and the NUMBER of ftates within it, vaftly increafe the difficulty of any political diforder diffufing its contagion, and the probability of its being repreffed ?

From the annals of mankind, thefe conclufions are deducible—that confederated ftates may act prudently and honeftly, and apart foolifhly and knavifhly; but, that it is a defiance

of all probability, to fuppofe, that ftates conjointly fhall act with folly and wickednefs, and
yet feparately with wifdom and virtue.

FABIUS.

LETTER VIII.

THE propofed confederation offers to us a fyftem of diverfified reprefentation, in the legiflative, executive, and judicial departments, as effentially neceffary to the good government of an extenfive republican empire. Every argument to recommend it, receives new force, by contemplating events, that muft take place. The number of ftates in *America* will encreafe. If not united to the prefent, the confequences are evident. If united, it muft be by a plan that will communicate *equal liberty* and affure *juft protection* to them. Thefe ends can never be attained, but by *a clofe combination* of the feveral ftates.

It has been afferted, that a very extenfive territory cannot be ruled by a government of republican form. What is meant by this propofition? Is it intended to abolifh all ideas of connection, and to precipitate us into the miferies of divifion, either as fingle ftates, or partial confederacies? To ftupify us into defpondence, that deftruction may certainly feize us? The fancy of poets never feigned fo dire a *Metamorphofis*, as is now held up to us. The *Ægis* of their *Minerva* was only faid to turn men into ftones. This fpell is to turn "a band of brethren," into a monfter, preying on itfelf, and preyed upon by all its enemies.

If hope is not to be abandoned, common fenfe teaches us to attempt the beft means of prefervation. This is all that men can do, and this they ought to do. Will it be faid, that any kind of difunion, or a connection tending to it, is preferable to a firm union? Or, *is there any charm in that defpotifm*, which is faid, to be alone competent to the rule of fuch an empire? There is no *evidence of fact*, nor any *deduction of reafon*, that juftifies the affertion. It is true, that extenfive territory has in general been arbitrarily governed; and it is as true, that a number of republics, in fuch territory, *loofely connected*, muft inevitably rot into defpotifm.

It is faid—Such territory has never been governed by a confederacy of republics. Granted. But, where was there ever a confederacy of republics, in fuch territory, united, *as thefe ftates are to be* by the propofed conftitution? Where was there ever a confederacy, in which, the fovereignty of each ftate was *equally reprefented* in one legiflative body, the people of each ftate *equally reprefented* in another, and the fovereignties and people of all the ftates *conjointly reprefented*, poffeffed fuch a qualified and temperating authority in making laws? Or, in which, the appointment to federal offices was vefted in a chief magiftrate *chofen* as our prefident is to be? Or, in which, the acts of the executive department were *regulated*, as they are to be with us? Or, in which, the federal judges were to hold their offices *independently* and *during good behaviour?* Or, in which, the authority over the militia and troops was *fo diftributed and controuled*, as it is to be with us? Or, in which, the people were *fo drawn together* by religion, blood, language, manners and

cuftoms, undifturbed by former feuds or prejudices? Or, in which, the affairs relating to the
whole union, were to be managed by an affembly of feveral reprefentative bodies, invefted
with different powers that became *efficient only
in concert*, without their being embarraffed by
attention to other bufinefs? Or, in which, a
provifion was made for the federal revenue,
without recurring to coercion againft ftates, the
miferable expedient of every other confederacy
that has exifted, an expedient always attended
with odium, and often with a delay productive of irreparable damage? Where was there
ever a *confederacy*, that thus adhered to *the firft
principle in civil fociety*; obliging by *its direct
authority* every individual, to contribute, when
the public good neceffarily required it, a juft
proportion of aid to the fupport of the commonwealth protecting him—*without difturbing
him in the difcharge of the duties owing by him to
the ftate of which he is an inhabitant*; and at
the fame time, fo amply, fo anxioufly provided, for bringing the interefts, and even the
wifhes of *every fovereignty* and of *every perfon*
of the union, under all their various modifica-
tions and impreffions, into their full operation
and efficacy in the national councils? The inftance never exifted. The conclufion ought
not to be made. It is without premifes. So
far is the affertion from being true, that " a very extenfive territory cannot be ruled by a government of a republican form," that fuch a
territory cannot be well-ruled by a government
of any other form.

The affertion has probably been fuggefted by reflections on the democracies of antiquity, without making a proper diftinction between them and the democracy of *The United States*.

In the democracies of antiquity, the people affembled together and governed *perfonally*. This mode was incompatible with greatnefs of number and difperfion of habitation.

In the democracy of *The United States*, the people act by their *reprefentatives*. This improvement collects the will of millions upon points concerning their welfare, with more advantage, than the will of hundreds could be collected under the ancient form.

There is another improvement equally deferving regard, and that is, the *varied reprefentation* of fovereignties *and* people in the conftitution now propofed.

It has been faid, that this reprefentation was a mere compromife.

It was not a mere compromife. THE EQUAL REPRESENTATION OF EACH STATE IN ONE BRANCH OF THE LEGISLATURE, was an original fubftantive propofition, made in convention, very foon after the draft offered by *Virginia*, to which laft mentioned ftate *United America* is much indebted not only in other refpects, but for her merit in the origination and profecution of this momentous bufinefs.

The propofition was *exprefsly* made upon *this principle*, that a territory of fuch extent as that of *United America*, could not *be fafely and advantageoufly governed*, but by a *combination* of republics, each *retaining* all the rights of fupreme fovereignty, *excepting* fuch as ought to be con-tributed to the union ; that for the fecurer *pre-fervation* of thefe fovereignties, they ought to be reprefented in a body *by themfelves*, and with *equal fuffrage* ; and that they would be annihi-lated, if both branches of the legiflature were to be formed of reprefentatives of the people, in proportion to the number of inhabitants in each ftate.*

The principle appears to be well founded in reafon. Why cannot a very extenfive territory be ruled by a government of republican form ? They anfwered, becaufe its power muft languifh through diftance of parts. Granted; if it be not a " body by joints and bands having nou-rifhment miniftered and knit together." If it be fuch a body, the objection is removed. In-ftead of *fuch a perfect body*, framed upon *the principle that commands men to affociate, and fo-cieties to confederate; that, which by communicating and extending happinefs, correfponds with the gra-cious intentions of our maker towards us his crea-tures; what is propofed?* Truly, that the na-tural legs and arms of this body fhould be cut off, becaufe they are too weak, and their places fupplied by ftronger limbs of wood and metal.

---

* *Juftice* Blackftone *argues in like manner, af-ter admitting the* "expediency" *of titles of nobility.* " *It is alfo expedient that their owners fhould form an independent and feparate branch of the legifla-ture*"—*otherwife* " *their privileges would foon be borne down and overwhelmed.*" *Comment.* 2. 157.

Monarchs, it is said, are enabled to rule extensive territories, becaufe they fend viceroys to govern certain diftricts ; and thus the reigning authority is tranfmitted over the whole empire. Be it fo: But, what are the confequences? Tyranny, while the viceroys continue in fubmiflion to their mifters, and the diftraction of civil war befides, when they revolt, to which they are frequently tempted by the very circumftances of their fituation, as the hiftory of fuch governments indifputably proves.

America is, and will be, divided into feveral fovereign ftates, each poffeffing every power proper for governing *within its own limits for its own purpofes,* and alfo for acting *as a member of the union.*

They will be *civil* and *military* ftations, *conveniently planted* throughout the empire, with lively and regular communications. A ftroke, a touch upon any part, will be immediately felt by the whole. *Rome* famed for imperial arts, had a glimpfe of this great truth ; and endeavoured, as well as her hard-hearted policy would permit, to realize it in her COLONIES. They were miniatures of the capital : But wanted the *vital principle of fovereignty,* and were too fmall. They were melted down into, or overwhelmed by the nations around them. Were they now exifting, they might be called curious automatons—fomething like to our *living* originals. *Thefe,* will bear a remarkable refemblance to the mild features of *patriarchal* government, in which each fon ruled *his own houfehold,* and in *other matters* the whole family was directed by the common anceftor.

Will a people thus happily fituated, ever defire to exchange their condition, for fubjection
to an abfolute ruler; or can they ever look but
with veneration, or act but with deference to
that union, that alone can, under providence,
preferve them from fuch fubjection ?

Can any government be devifed, that will
be more fuited to citizens, who wifh for *equal
freedom* and *common profperity;* better calculated
for preventing corruption of manners ; for ad-
vancing the improvements that endear or adorn
life ; or that can be more conformed to the *underftanding,* to the *beft affections,* to the very
nature of MAN ? What harvefts of happinefs
may grow from the feeds of liberty that are
now fowing ? The cultivation will indeed
demand continual attention, unceafing diligence, and frequent conflict with difficulties :
but, to object againft the benefits offered to us
by our Creator, by excepting to the terms annexed, is a crime to be equalled only by its
folly.

Delightful are the profpects that will open to
the view of *United America*—her fons well prepared to defend their own happinefs, and ready
to relieve the mifery of others—her fleets formidable, but only to the unjuft—her revenue
fufficient, yet unoppreffive—her commerce af-
fluent, but not debafing—peace and plenty
within her borders—and the glory that arifes
from a proper ufe of power, encircling them.

Whatever regions may be deftined for fervi-
tude, let us hope, that fome portions of this
land may be bleffed with liberty ; let us be con-

vinced, that NOTHING SHORT OF SUCH AN UNION as has been propofed, can preferve the blelfing; and therefore let us be refolved to adopt it.

As to alterations, a little EXPERIENCE will caft more light upon the fubject, than a multitude of debates. Whatever qualities are poffeffed by thofe who object, they will have the candor to confefs, that they will be encountered by opponents, not in any refpect inferior, and yet differing from them in judgment, upon every point they have mentioned.

Such untired induftry to ferve their country, did the delegates to the federal convention exert, that they not only laboured to form the beft plan they could, but, PROVIDED FOR MAKING AT ANY TIME AMENDMENTS ON THE AUTHORITY OF THE PEOPLE, without fhaking the ftability of the government. For this end, the Congrefs, whenever two-thirds of both houfes fhall deem it neceffary, fhall propofe amendments to the conftitution, or, on the application of the legiflatures of two-thirds of the feveral ftates, SHALL call a convention for propofing amendments, which, in either cafe, fhall be valid to all intents and purpofes, as part of the conftitution, when ratified by the legiflatures of three-fourths of the feveral ftates, or by conventions in three-fourths thereof, as one or the other mode of ratification may be propofed by Congrefs.

Thus, by a *gradual progrefs*, we may from time to time INTRODUCE EVERY IMPROVEMENT IN OUR CONSTITUTION, that fhall be fuitable to our fituation. For this purpofe, it may perhaps be advifeable, for every ftate, as it fees occafion, to form with the utmoft deliberation, drafts of alterations refpectively required by them, and to enjoin their reprefentatives, to employ every proper method to obtain a ratification.

In this way of proceeding, the undoubted fenfe of every ftate, collected in the cooleft manner, not the fenfe of individuals, will be laid before the whole union in congrefs, and that body will be enabled with the cleareft light that can be afforded by every part of it, and with the leaft occafion of irritation, to compare and weigh the fentiments of all *United America*; forthwith to adopt fuch alterations as are recommended by general unanimity; by degrees to devife modes of conciliation upon contradictory propofitions; and to give the revered advice of our common country, upon thofe, if any fuch there fhould be, that in her judgment are inadmiffible, becaufe they are incompatible with the happinefs of thefe ftates.

It cannot be with reafon apprehended, that Congrefs will refufe to act upon any articles calculated to promote the COMMON *welfare*, though they may be unwilling to act upon fuch as are defigned to advance PARTIAL *interefts:* but, whatever their fentiments may be, they MUST call a convention for propofing amendments, on applications of two-thirds of the legiflatures of the feveral ftates.

May thofe good citizens, who have fometimes turned their thoughts towards a fecond convention, be pleafed to confider, that there are men who fpeak as they do, yet do not mean as they do. Thefe borrow the fanction of their refpected names, to conceal defperate defigns. May they alfo confider, whether perfifting in the fuggefted plan, in preference to the conftitutional provifion, may not kindle flames of jealoufy and difcord, which all their abilities and virtues can never extinguifh.

FABIUS.

LETTER IX.

WHEN the fentiments of fome objectors, concerning the *Britifh* conftitution, are confidered, it is furprifing, that they fhould apprehend fo much danger to *United America*, as, they fay, will attend the ratification of the plan propofed to us, by the late federal convention.

These gentlemen will acknowledge, that *Britain* has fuftained many internal convulfions, and many foreign wars, with a gradual advancement in freedom, power, and profperity. They will acknowledge, that no nation has exifted that ever fo perfectly united thofe *diftant extremes*, private *fecurity of life, liberty, and property*, with *exertion of public force*—fo advantageoufly combined the various powers of militia, troops, and fleets—or fo happily blended together arms, arts, fcience, commerce, and agriculture. From what fpring has flowed this ftream of happinefs? The gentlemen will acknowledge, that thefe advantages are derived from *a fingle democratical branch in her legiflature.* They will alfo acknowledge, that in this branch, called the houfe of commons, only one hundred and thirty-one are members for counties: that nearly one half of the whole houfe is chofen by about five thoufand feven hundred perfons, moftly of no property; that fifty-fix members are elected by about three hundred and feventy

perfons, and the reft in an enormous difpro-
portion * to the numbers of inhabitants who
ought to vote. †

  Thus are all the millions of people in that
kingdom, faid to be reprefented in the houfe
of commons.

Let the gentlemen be fo good, on a fubject
fo familiar to them, as to make a comparifon
between the *Britifh* conftitution, and that propofed to us. Queftions like thefe will then
probably prefent themfelves : Is there more
danger to our liberty, from fuch a prefident as
we are to have, than to that of *Britons* from an
hereditary monarch with a vaft revenue—abfolute in the erection and difpofal of offices, and
in the exercife of the whole executive power—
in the command of the militia, fleets, and armies, and the direction of their operations—in
the eftablifhments of fairs and markets, the regulation of weights and meafures, and coining
of money—who can call parliaments with a
breath, and diffolve them with a nod—who
can, at his will, make war, peace, and treaties
irrevocably binding the nation—and who can

---

  * *No member of parliament ought to be elected
by fewer than the majority of* 800, *upon the moft
moderate calculation, according to Doctor* Price.

  † *By the conftitution propofed to us, a majority
of the houfe of reprefentatives, and of the fenate,
makes a quorum to do bufinefs : but, if the writer
is not miftaken, about a fourteenth part of the
members of the houfe of commons, makes a quorum
for that purpofe.*

L

grant pardons and titles of nobility, as it pleafes
him ? Is there more danger to us, from twenty-
fix fenators, or double the number, than to
Britons, from an hereditary ariftocratic body,
confifting of many hundreds, poffeffed of enormous wealth in lands and money——ftrengthened
by a hoft of dependants——and who, availing
themfelves of defects in the conftitution, fend
many of thefe into the houfe of commons——
who hold a third part of the legiflative power
in their own hands——and who form the higheft
court of judicature in the nation ? Is there more
danger to us, from a houfe of reprefentatives,
to be chofen by all the freemen of the union,
every two years, than to *Britons*, from fuch a
fort of reprefentation as they have in the houfe
of commons, the members of which, too, are
chofen but every feven years ? Is there more
danger to us, from the intended federal officers,
than to *Britons*, from fuch a monarch, ariftocracy, and houfe of commons together? WHAT
BODIES are there in *Britain*, vefted with fuch
capacities for enquiring into, ckecking, and
regulating the conduct of national affairs, AS
OUR SOVEREIGN STATES ? What proportion
does the number of FREEHOLDERS in *Britain*
bear to the number of people ? And what is
the proportion in *United America ?*
 If any perfon, after confidering fuch queftions, fhall fay, there will be more danger to our
freedom under the propofed plan, than to that
of *Britons* under their conftitution, he muft
mean, that *Americans* are, or will be, beyond
all comparifon, inferior to *Britons* in under-

ftanding and virtue; otherwife, with a conftitution and government, every branch of which
is fo extremely popular, they certainly might
guard their rights, at leaft as well, as *Britons*
can guard theirs, under fuch political inftitutions as they have; *unlefs the perfon has fome incli-*
nation to an opinion, that monarchy and ariftocracy
are favourable to the prefervation of their rights.
If he has, he cannot too foon recover himfelf.
If ever monarchy or ariftocracy appears in this
country, it muft be in the hideous form of defpotifm.

What an infatuated, depraved people muft
Americans become, if, with fuch unequalled
advantages, committed to their truft in a manner almoft miraculous, they lofe their liberty?
Through a fingle organ of reprefentation, in
the legiflature only, of the kingdom juft mentioned, though that organ is difeafed, fuch
portions of popular fenfe and integrity have
been conveyed into the national councils, as
have purified other parts, and preferved the
whole in its prefent ftate of healthfulnefs. To
their own vigour and attention, therefore, is
that people, under providence, indebted for
the bleffings they enjoy. They have held, and
now hold THE TRUE BALANCE in their government. While they retain their enlightened fpirit, they will continue to hold it; and IF THEY
REGARD WHAT THEY OWE TO OTHERS, as
well as what they owe to themfelves, they
will, moft probably, continue to be happy.*

---

* *If to the union of* England *and* Scotland, *a*
juft connection with Ireland *be added, ecclefiaftical*

They know, that there are powers that cannot be *exprefsly limited*, without injury to themfelves ; and their magnanimity fcorns any fear
of fuch powers. This magnanimity taught
Charles the firft, that he was but a royal fervant;
and this magnanimity caufed *James* the fecond's
army, raifed, paid, and kept up by himfelf,
to confound him with huzzas for liberty.

They afk not for compacts, of which the
national welfare, and, in fome cafes, its exiftence, may demand violations. They defpife
fuch dangerous provifions againft danger.

They know, that *all powers* whatever, even
thofe that, according to the forms of the con-

---

*eftablifhments duly amended, additions to the peer-
age regulated, and reprefentation of the commons
properly improved, it is to be expected, that the
tranquility, ftrength, reputation, and profperity of
the empire will be greatly promoted. The monarchy
will probably change into a republic, if reprefentation in the houfe of commons is not en-
creafed by additions from the counties and great
trading cities and towns. Without this precaution,
an increafe of the peerage feems likely to accelerate
an alteration. Thefe two meafures fhould have, it
is apprehended, in fuch a government and in fuch a
progrefs of human affairs, a well-tempered co-ope-
ration. The power of the crown might thereby
become more dignified, moderated, and fecured.*

*The difcuffion of this fubject would embrace a
very great number of confiderations ; but the conclufion feems to approach as near to demonftration,
as an inveftigation of this kind can do.*

ftitution, are irrefiftible and abfolute, of which
there are many, *ought to be exercifed for the public
good ;* and that when they are ufed to the public
detriment, they are unconftitutionally exerted.

This plain text, commented upon by their experienced intelligence, has led them fafe through
hazards of every kind : and *they now are, what
we fee them.* Upon the review, one is almoft
tempted to believe, that their infular fituation,
foil, climate, and fome other circumftances,
have compounded a peculiarity of temperature,
uncommonly favourable to *the union of reafon
and paffion.*

Certainly, 'tis very memorable, with what
life, impartiality, and prudence, they have interpofed on great occafions ; have by their patriotifm communicated temporary foundnefs to
their difordered reprefentation ; and have bid
public confufions to ceafe. Two inftances out
of many may fuffice. The excellent *William*
the third was diftreffed by a houfe of commons.
He diffolved the parliament, and appealed to
the people. They relieved him. His fucceffor,
the prefent king, in the like diftrefs, made the
fame appeal ; and received equal relief.

Thus *they* have acted : but *Americans*, who
have the fame blood in their veins, have, it
feems, very different heads and hearts. *We*
fhall be enflaved by a prefident, fenators, and
reprefentatives, chofen by ourfelves, and continually rotating within the period of time affigned for the continuance in office of members
in the houfe of commons ? 'Tis ftrange : but,
we are told, 'tis true. It may be fo. As we

have our all at ftake, let us enquire, in what way this event is to be brought about. Is it to be before or after a general corruption of manners? If after, it is not worth attention. The lofs of happinefs then follows of courfe. If before, how is it to be accomplifhed? Will a virtuous and fenfible people choofe villains or fools for their officers? Or, if they fhould choofe men of wifdom and integrity, will thefe lofe both or either, by taking their feats? If they fhould, will not their places be quickly fupplied by another choice? Is the like derangement again, and again, and again, to be expected? Can any man believe, that fuch aftonifhing phænomena are to be looked for? Was there ever an inftance, where rulers, thus felected by the people from their own body, have, in the manner apprehended, outraged their own tender connexions, and the interefts, feelings, and fentiments of their affectionate and confiding countrymen? Is fuch a conduct more likely to prevail in this age of mankind, than in the darker periods that have preceded? Are men more difpofed now more than formerly, to prefer uncertainties to certainties, things perilous and infamous to thofe that are fafe and honourable? Can all the myfteries of fuch iniquity, be fo wonderfully managed by treacherous rulers, that none of their enlightened conftituents, nor any of their honeft affociates, acting with them in public bodies, fhall ever be able to difcover the confpiracy, till at laft it fhall burft with deftruction to the whole federal conftitution? Is it not *ten thoufand times lefs probable*, that fuch tranfactions will happen, than it is, that we fhall be expofed to innumerable calamities, by rejecting the plan propofed, or even by delaying to accept it?

Let us confider our affairs in another light. Our difference of government, participation in commerce, improvement in policy, and magnitude of power, can be no favourite objects of attention to the Monarchies and Sovereignties of *Europe*. Our lofs will be their gain—our fall, their rife—our fhame, their triumph. Divided, they may diftract, dictate, and deftroy. United, their efforts will be waves dafhing themfelves into foam againft a rock. May our national character be—an *animated moderation*, that feeks only its own, and will not be fatisfied with lefs.

To his beloved fellow-citizens of *United America*, the writer dedicates this imperfect teftimony of his affection, with fervent prayers, for a perpetuity of freedom, virtue, piety, and felicity, to them and their pofterity.

F A B I U S.

THE

LETTERS

OF

FABIUS,

IN

1797.

M

THE

LETTERS

OF

FABIUS:

CONTAINING,

REMARKS on the PRESENT SITUATION

OF

PUBLIC AFFAIRS.

LETTER I.

TO publifh a few obfervations on the prefent fituation of public affairs, appears to me to be my duty. Under that impreffion to forbear, would be criminal.

Some of my countrymen want no information that I can give them. To thefe, it would be prefumption to offer it. Others perhaps have lefs favourable opportunities of obtaining information than I have had. To thefe I addrefs what I have now to fay.

Neither time, nor my infirmities will permit me to be attentive to ftyle, arrangement, or the labour of confulting former publications. I write from my heart—and from recollection.

Having nothing to hope, wifh, or fear, but as a commoner of 'thefe ftates, to which I am bound by birth, the tendereft pledges, friendfhips, and fellow-citizenfhip, I may be miftaken: but, I can never mean to deceive. My beft interefts of every kind are ranged againft the attempt. All that can be dear to man, is wrapp'd up for me, in the general welfare.

I know, and I refpect the formidable hoft I fhall provoke. My motives fortify me. I will provoke, becaufe I efteem them.

After our Revolution, two dangers prefented themfelves to view—*Internal difcord*, and *the jealoufy of foreign powers* refpecting the form of our government, efpecially if it fhould be *remarkably profperous*, which, no doubt, would be our defire and aim.

Any perfon acquainted with our tranfactions, in the two wars about the middle of this century, might eafily judge what was to be expected from *internal difcord*.

Our firft federal conftitution partook largely of the diffociating ingredients, that were too redundant among us. It was pregnant with diforders.

In 1787, the moft immediate evils of it, were in an extraordinary manner removed.

In 1788, the new conftitution commenced its operations, and held its courfe with an attendant affemblage of great benefits.

In the next year, furprizing political move-
ments began in *France*, apparently aufpicious
to the caufe of liberty and the interefts of mankind.

In the following years, the atmofphere was
obfcured by dark clouds. The neighbouring
powers, with fome remote, entered into a confederacy againft *France*. *There*, all the paffions of the foul were roufed. Perils from
without, perils from within diftracted the underftanding, and convulfed humanity. The
felfifh, the audacious, and the unfeeling feized
the difaftrous opportunity, and by plaufible
pretenfions to patriotifm clutch'd the public
opinion, and with it the public force.

The nation had a choice of difficulties. One
was, to embroil and weaken themfelves, by
contefts in the difpofal of power, and thus
more and more expofe themfelves to their formidable invaders. The other was, to adhere to
their leaders, however exceptionable their character and conduct, and thus make up as much
ftrength as they could, to repel their inexo-
rable enemies, referving better regulations for
more quiet and fafe times. They chofe the
laft, and as *we* did in a fimilar ftruggle,
bore many things that were wrong, rather
than difturb the exertions for general defence.

The tempeft raged with unceafing fury, and
in the midft of its direful glares, among vaft
crowds immolated with deteftable iniquity, a
facrifice rather to the policy of his pretended
friends, than to the hatred of *France*, fell—one
of the beft of kings, probably of men—the be-

nevolent *Louis* the XVI. whofe virtues I fhall value, whofe memory I fhall revere, whofe fate I fhall deplore, as long as any fenfe of efteem, refpect, and compaffion, embalmed by gratitude, fhall reft within the unbroken urn of my heart.

At length—the reign of tyrants, or rather of monfters, ended.

The agitations of *our* minds during thefe conflicts, were violent. Some among us were fo overheated, that they even vindicated the moft enormous atrocities of the moft abandoned of men, as neceffary feverities. But—this was not the fentiment of *America*. For every particle of needlefs violence, fhe fighed. She perceived the name of liberty profaned, the caufe difhonored, the interefts violated. What could fhe do amidft the rapid horrors? She pitied—detefted—wept—and execrated.

Through the murky exhalations from a bleeding land, a ray of hope twinkled. Soon afterwards the profpect brightened; and when the fky became clear, with tranfports of joy we faw *France* firm at her poft, and true to herfelf, to freedom, and to mankind.

Do *we* cenfure her, for enduring the horrible defpotifm of *the monfters*, during the paroxyfm of her deftiny, and not give her credit, for putting, as foon as circumftances permitted, a period to them and to their abominations? That would not be fair-dealing.

Her fubmiffion to them was proportioned to the foreign efforts to deftroy her. Thefe com-

pelled her, these impofed upon her a neceffity
to fubmit. How ? By a combination of almoft all *Europe*, againft a fingle nation in a
new and untried ftate, proclaiming " threats of
fire and fword," and labouring to execute thofe
threats, by the moft numerous and beft difcip-
lined armies, commanded by the moft renowned
generals in the world.

But—who affifted her to extinguifh *the fyftem
of terror ?* Any emperor, king, or prince ?
Any of the crowned profeffors, protectors,
and practifers of " *morality and religion ?*"
No. What then ? Her own good fenfe, fpirit, and humanity. THIS GLORIOUS ACT
WAS ALL HER OWN.

It was an act congenial to the feelings of
Frenchmen. Univerfal France—the mifcreants
of murder and pillage are too inconfiderable to
be regarded—univerfal *France* rejoiced in the
deed. Read the accounts written by foreigners
who were witneffes of the public exultations
upon the event. There one may find fome
traces of *French* mind.

The nation revived. She flung off her enemies from her frontiers, into their own territories. Thither fhe purfued them, as fhe had
a right to do. The war blazed. Her victories
were brilliant. She had declared herfelf a
REPUBLIC, was evidently competent to the
final eftablifhment of her liberty, and in that
attitude ftanding upon her trophies, ftretched
out her right hand to us, and proffered us her
friendfhip.

Thus the *second* danger before mentioned was enervated, if a harmony founded on good difpofitions towards one another and mutual interefts, could be accomplifhed.

FABIUS.

APRIL 10, 1797.

LETTER II.

IN order to eſtimate the value of a cordial amity with *France*, it may be worth while to conſider, on what foundation her ſtrength ſtands.

Her ſituation is moſt advantageous ; the ſoil is fertile ; its products are excellent ; the extent of coaſts on the ocean and the Mediterranean, and her rivers, inſure to her a flouriſhing commerce, and a vaſt maritime power. Her population is prodigious. Before the preſent war it amounted, at a moderate computation, to twenty-five millions. If to this ſum be added that of the conquered countries, which in all probability will be ceded to her at a peace, the whole, it is apprehended, muſt exceed thirty millions. Induſtry, vivacity, ingenuity, knowledge, and bravery, with the animating and invigorating principle of broad-baſed repreſentation, give to this population the utmoſt reſpectability.

The other day, in turning over *Polybius*'s celebrated hiſtory, my attention was arreſted by an unexpected enumeration in his ſecond book, of the forces of the commonwealth of *Rome*, when ſhe had attained to the higheſt pitch of power, juſt before *Hannibal*'s invaſion. The detail is very preciſe as to numbers and the countries that ſupplied them. His concluſion is this—" *the whole of their ſtrength* conſiſted in no leſs, than ſeven hundred thouſand infantry, and ſeventy thouſand cavalry."

N

Among the particulars, he mentions " the ordinary people muftered in *Rome* and *Campania*, amounting to two hundred and fifty thoufand foot, and twenty-three thoufand horfe." Thefe, if I underftand him rightly, were not armed for immediate fervice, but might be called upon, if occafions required their aid. Therefore, thefe words, " *the whole of their ftrength*," appear to mean all the perfons able to bear arms.

I believe, that the learned, in their calculations allow, that on an average, in a number of five or fix perfons, one will be found to be an able bodied man. Let a rule much more reftrictive be applied, for determining the number of men able to bear arms in *France*, and the refult will be, that their nnmber is four times as great as that mentioned by the hiftorian.

This is a gigantic power indeed. If it appears tremendous to fome, let them amufe their fancies, if they pleafe, with whittling it down as much as they can : but, let them not forget, that *France* has actually employed in military fervice, in one year, nearly double the number of the total before mentioned. Let us go further. Let us ftrike off one half of the complement which fair calculation gives us. Still it remains a fact fufficiently afcertained, that the ftrength of *France* is at this moment, twice as great as that of *Rome* in the plenitude of her power at the period mentioned.

Nor is the comparifon to be difmiffed with this obfervation, unlefs we are willing to deceive ourfelves. To follow it out, another circumftance muft be confidered.

Of the seven hundred and seventy thousand men just spoken of, scarcely a moiety was composed of *Romans*. The rest were *allies*, of which an exact catalogue is given in the history.

These *allies* were nations, who by various motives were induced to join the *Romans* in arms; but, so imperfect was the connection, that not long after, a fierce war broke out between these *allies* and the *Romans*, that brought the last to the brink of destruction.

The power of *France* leans not on such ill-matched supporters. Her power is *native*, and not attenuated by being dispersed in a long, narrow country like *Italy*,* with rivers comparatively of slight importance, but bound together in a compactness blended with facilities, equally propitious to intercourse and consolidation. It is an *Herculean* body, of strength and activity—unparalleled in the history of mankind.

It may be said, that " the power of states is relative : a mighty power may be encountered by mightier powers." Granted.

At the time I am speaking of, proud and warlike *Macedon* was a formidable kingdom. *Greece*, famed for arts and arms, abounded with sensible and gallant men. The *Syrian* empire was large and strong. *Gaul*, the former victor of *Rome*, was dreadful.——Above all—with one foot fixed on *Africa*, and the other on *Spain*, the genius of CARTHAGE, like a

---

* Italy *is spoken of here, as it was before the name was extended to other countries.*

ſtupendous coloſſus, beſtrode the ſea, waving his terrific flag over its ſubject billows, and in a voice of thunder, imperiouſly dictating law, hard law, to nations.

All theſe, in their turns, *ſeparately* became enemies to *Rome*; and in their turns, all the " *lions, bears, leopards, rams,* and *goats*".* bowed before her irreſiſtible *birds*.† The *Euxine*, the *Caſpian*, the *Perſian-gulf*, and the *Ocean*, were made the boundaries of her dominions.

Againſt *France* we have ſeen, *all at once* combined, *Ruſſia, Pruſſia, Auſtria, Germany, The United Provinces, Belgium, Britain, Spain, Sardinia,* and *Italy.*

How ſhe has diſpoſed of ſome of theſe adverſaries, and how ſhe has diſabled others of them, we very well know. What further *proof* of her puiſſance ſhe may exhibit, time will ſhew : but, if we are to judge of the future from the paſt, which perhaps is a good way of judging in ſuch caſes, it will not be hereafter any more than it has been already, only what the lawyers call a " *ſemi plena probatio,*" a half proof. It will be *full* and *deciſive.*

F A B I U S.

---

* Daniel, *chapters 7th and 8th.*

† The Romans *took for their emblem an* Eagle, *a homely, ſolitary, ſilent bird of prey, never celebrated for its temper or its battles. With a much happier fancy, the* cock *has been aſſigned to the* French, *a beautiful, ſocial, ſprightly, generous, good-natured bird, that crows and fights, and, if over-matched, dies———ſtruggling for victory.*

LETTER III.

"IS *France* then to become as dominating as ancient *Rome?*". I do not know. I hope she never will. But, this I am much inclined to believe, that if she ever becomes so, it will be owing to the miferable policy, that forbidding her to return into the bofom of peace, and to enjoy the ineftimable and tranquilizing plea-fures of civil and domeftic life, adds irritation to irritation, and *obliges* her to be a MILITA-RY REPUBLIC, as *Rome* was. It is evident to me, that on the pureft principles, she wifhes for peace; but is convinced she cannot obtain it, unlefs it be by the fword.

"Can *France* wifh for peace, when she makes fuch exorbitant demands?"

Yes. Multitudes of her citizens have been flain; many fevere calamities have been inflict-ed upon her; and she has been put to an expence hardly to be calculated. Why? Becaufe she was refolved to be free, and to " inftitute fuch a government, as to her feemed moft likely to effect her fafety and happinefs."* She had a

---

* "*We hold thefe truths to be felf-evident; that all men are created equal; that they are endowed by their Creator with certain unalienable rights; that among thefe are life, liberty, and the purfuit of happinefs; that to fecure thefe rights, Governments are inftituted among men, deriving their juft powers from the confent of the governed; that whenever any government becomes deftruEtive of thefe ends,*

right to be free ; and to inftitute fuch a go-vernment. What right then had the coalefced princes to interfere in the bufinefs ? None. But they did interfere. She has therefore two other rights fpringing up from that injuftice : a right to indemnification, and a right to fecu-rity againft a repetition of fuch injuries.

"Suppofing, fhe has thofe rights, ftill her demands are exorbitant, and if admitted, would deftroy the balance of power, and endanger the welfare of *Europe*."

As to the firft part of this obfervation, it may be fufficient to obferve, that when *we* were treating of peace with *Great-Britain*, our demands were thought exorbitant ; and they have been thought fo fince : but, we obtained them. The charge of exorbitancy is eafily made, but not eafily to be maintained. The fitnefs of the ap-plication to any particular cafe, muft depend upon a number of peculiar circumftances, and feveral of thefe perhaps cannot be by foreigners, accurately inveftigated or properly eftimated.

France is in poffeffion by conqueft, in a juft war, a war of defence, for the machinations againft her were prior to her declarations. She is the only republic attracting confideration in

---

it is the right of the people to alter or abolifh it, and to inftitute new government, laying its founda-tion on fuch principles, and organizing its powers in fuch form, as to them fhall feem moft likely to effect their fafety and happinefs."

Declaration of INDEPENDENCE by The United States of America,

Europe. She is detested by most if not all the princes in that quarter of the world. There is not a nation there, in whose good will towards her she can confide. She must take care of her-self; she ought to do it; and she will do it: whatever exclamations are made about exorbi-tancy. Nor is there a great power in *Europe*, in whose hands the objects comprehended in her demands would be more favourable to ge-neral welfare, than in her hands.

She has made peace with several of the bel-ligerent powers, upon reasonable and moderate terms. This behaviour evinces her temper; and if nations had more command of *their own tem-pers* than they now have, they would render more justice than they do, to the character of *France*. They will be undeceived, and most heartily do I wish, that the explanation may not be delayed. 'Tis time the tragedy should end, and that men should look at one another for other purposes, than to aim weapons of destruction.

I am addressing men of sense and integrity, real *Americans*. They know, they feel, that the spirit of liberty is a benign spirit—From *them* a sacred impartiality—*sacred*, because min-gled with sensibilities allied to Heaven—may be expected.

Let any one of these lay his hand on his breast, and upon *the honour of a freeman*, answer this question——Whether, if conspiring em-pires, kingdoms, and states, actuated by a ha-tred unappeasable because arising from a conduct meriting esteem, had destroyed millions of our citizens, had rendered more millions of fathers, mothers, wives, children, fifters, brothers, and other relatives miferable, and had overwhelmed our country with a deluge of diftreffes,-he would think fuch *demands* as *France* is faid to make, a compenfation for our fufferings, or more than a reafonable fecurity againft a renewal of them ?

Let *us* remember, how *we* thought and acted on a fimilar occafion. What the *Miffifippi* and *The Lakes*, then were to us, the *Rhine* now is to *France*, with this difference, that our demands as to diftant objects went more to aggrandife-ment than defence, thofe of *France* more to de-fence than aggrandifement.

Would *we* have continued the war for thefe remote boundaries, this fweeping circuit within whofe flowing line fcarcely a trace was fketched of that beautiful picture which is to fill it, if we have fufficient fkill ? We would.

Is *France* then criminal, in contending for the *Rhine* as a boundary, a river that wafhes a long tract of her domain, is of immediate and the utmoft confequence to her, and is fo placed by nature as conveniently to ferve, among other ufes, for " dividing to nations their inheri-tance ?"

Well may our allies fay to their imperial, royal, and high enemies—" We have not been engaged in childrens' play, at the end of which each takes what was his own before it began. Our conteft may, indeed, have been play to you, iffuing mandates for flaughter amidft the fafe though foft indulgencies of your courts, and di-verted with expectations of lucky hits : but, to multitudes of *French* citizens it has been—death."

If it was on your part, as fome of you have faid, an unhappy diforder that feized you in an extraordinary manner, we ought to ob-ferve, that perfons in your elevated ftations are very apt to grow giddy, and to be much vexed by thefe fits of infanity ; and therefore prudence requires, that we fhould keep you at a conveni-ent diftance, left in another frolic or fury, you fhould deftroy as many men, women, and child-ren, as you have within thefe laft four years."

F A B I U S.

LETTER IV.

WE come to the fecond part of the objection.

If hereafter a wild fpirit of ambition, fhould
prompt *France* to imitate *Rome*, it will not be
her acquifitions of *The Netherlands* and countries
on the left bank of the *Rhine*, that will caufe her
to fucceed. What are *they*, when contrafted
with all *Europe?* The event of fuch a nefarious
project, would not depend on that point. If it
could not be executed without that acceffion, it
could not be executed with it.

There are other circumftances that would be
much more likely to give it fuccefs : and thefe
are the follies and vices of princes.

Caft your eyes around, and behold the condition of the human race—a condition, that while
it evidences their wretchednefs, and extorts your
commiferation, yet amidft *the Ruins of Man*,
bears teftimony to the *original glories* of his nature,
" whofe *builder* is GOD."

How have men, " made in the image of their
Creator," become thus depreffed ? Becaufe their
difpofition is gentle, focial, grateful, well-mean-
ing, and therefore confiding.

Thefe qualities they rafhly indulged, not duly
attending to another divine gift——REASON
—the guide and guardian of the Microcofm.

No gift of our Maker can be neglected or
abufed with impunity. His laws are not made,
to be broken.

The cunning, the hard-hearted, laden with
lufts, availed themfelves of the means afforded

to them by the innocent and the imprudent.
They affected to be benefactors that they might
be masters. They were too fuccefsful. *They*
faftened chains upon the hands that were held
up to Heaven in fupplication for bleffings upon
their heads. The interefts of the *many*, pleafing
hecatombs in the religion of governors, have
been facrificed to the paffions of the *few*. Tyranny and flavery, intemperance and mifery
have raged and are now raging, over the globe.

To nations thus fleeped in woes, when liberty advances towards them, " the trumpet
may give an uncertain found"—but, when they
" underftand it they will prepare themfelves for
the battle"—*unlefs juftice be rendered them*.

THE BALANCE OF POWER fo much talked
of, is generally a compact between the oppreffors of mankind, fettling among themfelves,
the quantity of mifchief which each may com-
mit, without being difturbed by the reft : and
I appeal to hiftory for the truth of what I now
fay. We have had a fample, in our own days,
of this attention to the balance of power——IN
THE PARTITION OF POLAND——by
which a noble nation was defpoiled of liberty,
at the very moment when they were moft fenfible of its value : a deed, as bafe and as cruel
as any, the records ancient or modern of tyrannical hoftilities againft the human race, can
fupply.

I have faid *generally*, becaufe there have been
fome wife and commendable efforts, to maintain a balance of power in *Europe*. I have in
my recollection, the alliances formed in the be-

ginning of the feventeenth century, and continued to the peace of *Munfter*, near the middle
of it, for controuling the power of the houfe
of *Auftria*; and thefe alliances were crowned
with fuccefs. I have alfo in my recollection,
the alliances formed afterwards in that century,
and renewed about the beginning of this, for
controuling the power of the houfe of *Bourbon*,
and thefe alliances too were crowned with fuccefs.

Thefe were manly, generous exertions, meriting to fucceed, and may all fuch exertions
have a like iffue. Should *France* ever adopt
the principles that were adopted by the heads
of thofe houfes, fhe will become as deteftable
as they have been and now are, and will deferve to be with them condemned to everlafting
infamy.

What did thefe houfes, the exalted artificers
of evils, the illuftrious difturbers of the earth
gain, by all their policy and all their guilt, all
their frauds and all their outrages? Solid mifery for *their affectionate people*; for *themfelves*,
one of them a fhattered empire, the contempt
of thofe they once contemned, and a long account of debits, the payment of which is now
in a train of exaction: and the other of them
provinces and fortreffes, whofe projecting im-
pediments and terrors now forbid their pofterity even to behold their native land.

" *Difcite juftitiam, moniti, et non temnere*" *Deum*—
Take warning—revere juftice—and defpife not
the ruler of the Univerfe.

F A B I U S.

LETTER V.

IF *France*, in a delirium of intoxication, should ever aim at the subjugation of *Europe*, or a great part of it, what will prevent such alliances being formed against her, as have heretofore put a stop to the aggressions of her monarchs? To others, the cause will be, as it was then, energetically cementing. Each will know, that his liveliest hope without such alliances is only—to be the last devoured. What will hinder such alliances from being as successful as former ones?—Will there not be as much force in them, as there was in the preceding? There will be, and a greater force, * if they are formed with the same prudence and fidelity.

The late successes of *France* offer no proof to the contrary. The confederacy against her, was framed on criminal and discordant principles. *Criminal,* because its views were—*dismemberment,* and *compulsion to slavery,* As soon as some of the confederates enlightened by irresistible arguments discovered, that the scheme was hopeless, or at least that the candle was of more value than the game, they closed the tables.

The principles were *discordant* too. There was no point of union, as in the laudable alliances before mentioned. The associates were

---

* *Several countries in* Europe *have encreased in power since the last century, much more than* France *has done.*

not fighting for their *common fafety*, unfpeakably interefting and impulfive to all, but each for his peculiar fhare of *plunder*. Some of them found out, that they did not ftand fo good a chance in this brigandage, as others. In this hunt with lions, the ftrongeft were likely to take all the prey to themfelves, and their companions to fit down at the end of it, hungry, weary, lacerated, and licking their wounds. Thefe accordingly left the chace, and betook themfelves to a better employment.

In thefe refpects, the confederacy was defect-ive.

Again—the principal operations were at the frontiers of *France*. This circumftance gave her great advantages; efpecially if fhe could caft the war, as fhe did, into neighbouring countries of her enemies. Her domeftic re-fources were within reach. Contributions aid-ed them. This is a cafe very different, from that of traverfing remote, hoftile regions, of climates diffimilar to her own, abounding with difficulties of paffage, and filled with warlike and enraged inhabitants. She has experienced the obftinacy of fuch obftructions, whenever her armies have entered far into *Germany*.

Look at the map of *Europe*, and fee the pro-portion which *France* bears to the whole of it. Examine any treatife upon the comparative po-pulation of the different countries. I don't pre-tend to be exact, but, I believe, none of them eftimates the population of *France*, at more than one-fifth of the aggregate. Many of thefe na-tions have a redundancy of all the materials re-

quifite for the manufacture of arms, and underftand the art of war as well as the *French*. If
their countries fhall be invaded, why fhould
not *they* feel the fame paffions excited, and refift
as firmly as the *French* did, when their country
was invaded ? It will not be faid, I prefume,
that they will have LESS at ftake ; for, if the
French had MORE at ftake, *what was it ?* It
could not be foil or climate, though both are
delightful in *France :* for every nation appears
to be fo well reconciled to its own, as to prefer it to that of others, and it is not a fiction
of the poet, when he fays—

    " *What happier nature fhrinks at with affright,*
    " *The hard inhabitant contends is right.*"

If I am not miftaken, fome learned and ingenious men, natives of the northerly and rugged-
eft parts of *Europe*, have written books to prove
them to be the moft charming of the earth.
What MORE then had the *French* to contend
for, than other nations of *Europe* would have,
upon an invafion ?—Whatever IT was, fince it
produced fuch ardor and perfeverance in the defence of their country, humanity muft dictate a
wifh to benevolent minds, that every other nation may have THE SAME animating and invigorating object before them.

  Neither will it be faid, I prefume, that the
French are braver than the other nations of *Europe*. If it fhould be faid, it is not neceffary
to controvert the affertion. This feems plain,
that if they *are*, their friendfhip is worth
cultivating.

Other caufes for the feceffion of fome of the confederates mixed with thofe already mentioned.

The hereditary averfions of *Spain* and *Pruffia*, covered over for a while with deceitful afhes fince blown off, again began to glow. By the firft, *Gibraltar* and *Jamaica* could not be forgot. *Corfica* as the front door, and the *Weft India* iflands at the back door, feized by *Great-Britain*, afforded new matter for meditation.

Pruffia might acquire more by friendfhip with *France*, whofe potency was now indifputable, than by the ill-concocted and ever-fufpected amity of *Auftria*. At leaft it was no inconfiderable point to fave men and money, while her ancient enemy was profufely wafting both. HAPPILY FOR HER, SHE WAS NOT SO BLINDED WITH PASSION, AS TO BE INCAPABLE OF DISCERNING HER TRUE INTEREST.

What a pity ! that a confederacy formed for fuch glorious purpofes, as the prefervation of the balance of power in *Europe*, her general welfare, and ftill more—for the prefervation of " *morality and religion*," fhould be forfaken for fuch inferior and fhameful confiderations ! Yet, fo it has been, and fo it ever will be, while the rulers of mankind, holding out fpecious pretences to deceive the too credulous world, are only devifing leagues for the gratification of their own inordinate defires. Piques, jealoufies, intrigues and temptations of partial advantage, will be continually fracturing a coalition, that has no found attracting principle of adhefion : or in other words, the fame vicioufnefs of difpofition that generated it, will infallibly deftroy it. "A corrupt tree *cannot* bring forth good fruit."

When the principle is right, the effect is directly the reverfe.

From thefe premifes may we not juftly infer, that, if the domination of *France* fhall be really apprehended by *Europe*, fhe poffeffes adequate means of defence?

That it is really apprehended does not appear to be the cafe at prefent: but, on the contrary, the eftablifhment of fuch a republic as *France*, will beam with an aufpicious afpect on mankind. Who that is the leaft acquainted with their fituation, but muft ardently wifh for its amelioration? In 1783, congrefs, in an addrefs to the citizens of thefe ftates, declared their expectation, that from *our* revolution, THE CAUSE OF LIBERTY would acquire a dignity and luftre which it had never yet enjoyed; and that an EXAMPLE would be fet which COULD NOT BUT HAVE the moft favourable influence on THE RIGHTS OF MANKIND." The "*example*" has been followed by the greateft people upon earth; and if fuch vaft benefits to our fellow-creatures could be produced by *our* conduct, how tranfcendant muft they be, that are to be expected from *republican France?*

The *governors* of nations if they do not learn humanity, will at leaft be taught to pay a greater refpect than they have been accuftomed to do, to the happinefs of the *governed*. They will be obliged *for their own fafety*, to communicate as much as they poffibly can of the bleffings

P

enjoyed by freemen, to thofe over whom they exercife authority. Republics cannot eafily be impoverifhed or fet a bleeding, by the rapacity, the pride, the rafhnefs, the ambition, or other vices of a few individuals. HEREDITARY RULERS MUST TAKE GREAT CARE, THAT THEY DO NOT GIVE CAUSE FOR DANGEROUS COMPARISONS.

For thefe reafons, and fuch others as a train of thought upon the fubject may fuggeft, it is apprehended, that thofe among us, who have fuppofed, that the eftablifhment of *France* as a republic, all her demands obtained, will give her an *unjuft* or *improper* elevation, may make up their minds with much fatisfaction.

FABIUS.

LETTER VI.

ANOTHER confideration of vaft magnitude in the prefent fituation of our affairs, is this—What *will be* the ftate of *France* at the termination of the war?

This confideration is of vaft magnitude to us, not that any one can be fo weak as to imagine, it can with prophetic certainty be foretold; but, becaufe if WE think *that* ftate will be unfavorable to her, WE may be led into moft pernicious miftakes.

A very ingenious and learned writer has told us, that " *France* will be obliged to return under the former defpotifm, or will be divided into a number of democratical republics."

If WE entertain the fame notion, perhaps we may act upon it. If we do, and it proves to be an error, even his abilities and knowledge, extraordinary as they are, will be perplexed to calculate the confequences.

The victories and conquefts of *France* have been defcribed in our news-papers. They need not be recapitulated.

" But—their armies have been frequently defeated."

So it has often happened to nations, that at the conclufion of wars have come off triumphant. So it was with us.

When an oppreffed nation draws the fword to affert her liberty, all the nobleft paffions, affections, and faculties are brought into ardent concentration. The collected rays that flafh'd from the glaffes of *Archimedes*, were not more irrefiftible. For inftances in point, I refer to *Rome* after the expulfion of the *Tarquins*, to *Switzerland*, to *The United Provinces*, and to *thefe States*. Any man, if but flightly acquainted with the workings of the human mind, in emotions where felfifhnefs expands to fanctity, cannot overlook this commanding temperament.—Whence derived, let thofe enquire, who doubt whether our adorable Maker loves his creatures of mankind, and approves their vindication of the rights, which blended with their reafon, he has been moft gracioufly pleafed to " *breathe*"* into their exiftence.

" But—there are multitudes of difaffected perfons in *France*, who wifh for peace at any rate."

So there were among us; and fo there have been, and will be in all nations under the like circumftances. *Great-Britain* trufting in fuch tales, was encouraged to continue the havoc of defolation in this land, till news more ftrange and true, baffled fleets and captured armies, convinced her that her reliance was illufion.

If a man had converfed with people in many parts of this country during our laft war, he might have been induced to believe, that *America* was ready for unconditional fubmiffion. But that would have been a miftake. The impulfe was given, and operating according to the laws of nature; but, it was looked for in wrong places: juft as if one fhould judge of

---

* *Genefis*, 2. 7.

the tide in a river by obſerving the eddies at its ſides, and believe it was running down, when in the channel it was flowing up with a ſtrong ſtream.

" It is ſaid—the finances of *France* are quite deranged."

She confeſſes it.

So are the finances of her enemies. They deny it. Yet—they beg for peace : ſhe prefers a continuance of the war. Let us put theſe things together : and————think.

" It is alſo ſaid—the war is continued, becauſe her rulers are averſe to peace, through fear of loſing their offices at its reſtoration."

That is to ſay, that men certainly of eminent talents, appointed by and dependant upon the people, with recent and terrible examples before them, would riſk their lives to ſave their poſts. The fact is, that *France* applauds the conduct of her government in breaking off the late negociation with *Great-Britain*, and ſo general and ſo warm is this ſentiment, that individuals who loudly arraigned the haughtineſs diſplayed at its commencement, with impaſſioned praiſes celebrate the firmneſs manifeſted in its diſſolution.

" It is further ſaid—if the armies ſhould be diſbanded, and the ſoldiers return to their homes, there will be a hideous exploſion."

That is to ſay—that bodies of men, who have given every demonſtration men could give, of PUBLIC SPIRIT and LOVE OF COUN TRY, when received with tranſports of gr titude on their natal ſoil, the ſweet reme brancer of their earliest and purest pleasures; where the tenderest affections shielded their helpless infancy, where all the charities of life with untutored eloquence plead their gentle rights, and where even every tree, stone, and brook claims kindred——will instantly be transformed into villains and traitors, and destroy those very objects, for the defence of which they had so long offered themselves——to die.

F A B I U S.

LETTER VII.

FROM thefe fables let us turn to hiftcry.

About two hundred and fixty years before the commencement of our æra, a war, of
fuch influence on the affairs of mankind, that
though twenty centuries of time have been fince
meafured out, yet every nation in *Europe* at this
day, feels impreffions from the event—broke
out between CARTHAGE and ROME.

The *Romans* had not then made any eftablifhment out of *Italy*. *Carthage* was poffeffed of
very large dominions in *Africa*, had made confiderable acquifitions in *Spain*, was fovereign
of *Sardinia*, *Corfica*, and all the iflands on the
coaft of *Italy*, and had extended her conquefts
to a great part of *Sicily*. She was then, and
had been for ages, unrivalled *miftrefs* of the
Mediterranean, the celebrated theatre of ancient
maritime adventure, and her navigation alone
bounded over the mountainous waves of the
ocean.

The *Romans* got out a fleet as well as they
could. But, fo inconfiderable was it in comparifon with that of the *Carthaginians*, and fo
unfkilful were they in naval tactics, that moft
of their fhips were taken, others dafhed in
pieces by a ftorm, and the battered remains retired to a port in *Italy*.

They had contrived to tranfport * an army

---

* POLYBIUS, *in his firft book, fays, that the*
ROMANS *were fo unprovided with fhipping for*

to *Sicily*, an ifland of vaft confequence to *Car-thage*, and there they were fuccefsful · but, they obferved, that the coafts of their own country lay expofed to the depredations of their enemies, who often made defcents upon them, while the dominions of the *Carthaginians* were in perfect tranquility. Refolved, therefore to be as formidable at fea as they were on land, they ordered one hundred *quinqueremes*, the fhips of the line in thofe days, and twenty *triremes*, equivalent to the frigates of modern times, to be built. So unexperienced were they, that a *Carthaginian* galley, which venturing too near the fhore had been ftranded and taken, was the model for this armament.

The *Romans* immediately fet about this labo-rious work, cut down trees in their forefts, and conveyed them to the fea fide, with an expedi-tion of which no example was known. The fleet was built and equipped in two months, reckoning from the day the trees began to be cut down.

While fome were employed in building the gallies, others affembling thofe who were to ferve on board, inftructed them in the ufe of the oar in the following odd manner. They conftructed benches on the fhore, in the fame fafhion and order as they were to be in the gallies, and placing the men on thefe benches, an officer by figns with his hand directed them

tranfporting this army, that they were obliged to borrow veffels from their neighbours for that pur-pofe.

how to dip all their oars at once, and with the like regularity to recover them. Thus they became acquainted with the management of the oar; and as foon as the veffels were finifhed and fitted out, they fpent fome time in practifing on the water what they had learned on fhore.

The exertions of the *Romans* on this occafion, appeared fo aftonifhing to *Polybius*, that they engaged him to undertake writing a hiftory of the war.

After various fuccefs, this fleet was almoft wholly deftroyed by a ftorm. The *Romans* got out another. That was deftroyed in like manner. They were fo much affected by thefe loffes, that it was decreed—that for the future no more than fifty veffels fhould be fent out, and that thefe fhould be employed only in guarding the coafts of *Italy*, and in tranfporting troops to *Sicily*.

After fome time, they refumed their ufual vigour, and put a new fleet to fea, knowing they could by no other means keep their hold of *Sicily*, fo important to them by its vicinity to *Italy*, and for other reafons. This fleet confifted of an hundred and twenty gallies. The *Carthaginians* with only ninety, met, defeated it, and took all the fhips but thirty.

Still undaunted and perfevering, the *Romans* fitted out another fleet of the fame force. The *Carthaginians* defpifing them fince the late defeat, failed out to fight it: but their pilots forefeeing that a ftorm was coming on, retired to a fafe harbour. The *Romans* not aware of the impending danger, kept the fea. The ftorm

Q

came on. The deftruction was total. Not a
fingle galley, not a fingle tranfport, and there
were eight hundred, with a large army on
board, and laden with all forts of provifions
and military ftores, efcaped.

The *Romans* now laid afide all thoughts of
building new gallies. The number of *Roman*
citizens appeared by a cenfus now taken, to be
reduced no lefs than 86,575 fince the laft cenfus
was taken.

However a large fleet of privateers was fitted
out, and the commonwealth lent to private perfons, *gratis*, the gallies fhe had left. Thefe
privateers acting together, obtained fome advantages over the *Carthaginians*; and committed great devaftations. They were afterwards
deftroyed by a ftorm.

The fteady *Romans* fitted out at the expence
of private perfons, to be reimburfed *when the
republic fhould be able*, another fleet. It confifted of two hundred *quinqueremes*. The new
armament far exceeded any of the former. It
was built on an improved model taken from
the *Carthaginians*. Thus, *at laft* well prepared
the *Romans* foon gained a complete victory; became mafters at fea, as well as on land : and
after a conteft of twenty-four years, in which
they loft feven hundred gallies, while their enemies loft only five hundred, made an honourable and advantageous peace, by which, all
their demands being obtained, among other
articles, *Sicily* and the iflands near to it and
Italy were yielded to them.

F A B I U S.

LETTER VIII.

OF all national powers, that which is chiefly derived from commercial resources, seems to be the most precarious. It depends too much on extraneous support. It must be exercised not only with great wisdom, but also with great virtue; that is, it must be beneficial to others, as well as profitable to the people possessing it, or it cannot be permanent. Our Creator never made individuals or nations, to be kind to themselves only. When attended with eminent success, it is apt to generate a spirit of pride, dissipation, insolence, rashness, rapaciousness, and cruelty. The eagerness for wealth, increases with amassment. It rages. It is a pestilence. Altered nations preserve scarcely a resemblance of themselves. Hardly a feature of their promising youth, remains in their debauched manhood. They, who were worthily diligent and decently frugal, become wickedly active and impudently avaricious: and, they who nobly defended their own liberty, deem it glorious to destroy the liberty of others. With them, justice is a restraint: Benevolence a weakness. To use an expression of *Thucydides*, " Nothing is thought dishonorable that is pleasing, nothing iniquitous that is gainful.

Let us bestow our attention for a moment, on *Athens*, *Carthage*, *Venice*, and *Holland*. Each of these states, by the force of commerce, has been predominant over considerable tracts of the world; and to each of them might many nations fay, with the old *Roman*——" *By our wretchednefs thou art great.*" Thus commerce calculated by its nature to be an inftrument for encreafing the felicity of mankind, has in many inftances become a fcourge.

If a conclufion may be drawn from a multitude of events delivered down to us by unprejudiced hiftorians, the monitory refult is—that the conduct juft mentioned will be found ultimately to produce confequences, directly the reverfe of the purpofes intended by the fhort-fighted perpetrators—and that where nations raife themfelves, by proudly trampling upon others, although they may by bravery, and management obtain the moft confpicuous eminence, yet, by THE IMMUTABLE LAW OF OUR NATURE THAT FORBIDS THE EXISTENCE OF HAPPINESS WITHOUT VIRTUE, the caufes of declenfion conftantly intermingle with their criminal fucceffes——" Grow with their growth and ftrengthen with their ftrength"—and at the period when their guilty glory reaches its greateft height, then piecifely are they near to their fall.*

* *How ftrictly conformable are fuch events to the divine denunciations in fo many parts of the Scriptures, againft national infolence and tyranny, of which the following texts may ferve for examples.*

" *Thus faith the* LORD GOD—*behold I am againft thee and will make thee moft defolate. I will lay thy city wafte, and thou fhalt be defolate; and thou fhall know that I am the* LORD. *Be-*

Each of the republics lately mentioned was deeply guilty. Could the murdered and the miferable, the victims of their crimes, rife from their beds of death, and move in filent proceffion before our eyes, we recollecting the delicacies, the virtues, the tender affections, the generous fenfations, that in their perfons had been violated and racked into the utmoft exacerbation of human woes—though confcious to ourfelves that their fufferings were paffed, how would our brains burn with anguifh, if floods of tears fhould not relieve us?

For what were thefe crimes committed? For no better purpofes than——

"To drink from gems and fleep on *Tyrian* dyes."

I had proceeded thus far in thefe letters, when the late advices from *Italy* came to my knowledge. How the actions there may influence the councils at *Vienna* and *London*, is uncertain,

---

cauſe thou haſt had a perpetual hatred, and haſt ſhed blood by the force of the ſword—becauſe thou haſt ſaid, theſe nations and theſe countries ſhall be mine, and we will poſſeſs them—therefore, as I live, ſaith the Lord God, I will do according to thine anger, and according to thine envy, which thou haſt uſed out of thy hatred againſt them—and thou ſhalt know that I am the Lord, and that I have heard all thy blaſphemies which thou haſt ſpoken—ſaying they are laid deſolate, they are given us to conſume—I have heard them—when the whole earth rejoiceth, I will make thee deſolate, and they ſhall know that I am the Lord.

Ezekiel 35.

My fervent defire is, that united with other confiderations they may fpeedily produce a peace
that will affure lafting tranquility and a large
abundance of benefits to *Europe*, and to all
parts of the world that have any kind of connection with any of her powers.

There is not a nation upon earth, whofe
welfare would not give me pleafure : And, as
I wifh, that the obfervations now offered to
my fellow-citizens, may not be impeached, at
a period fo momentous to my country as the
prefent, by a charge of prejudice in favor of
France, or of enmity to *Great-Britain*, I truft,
that by the candid I fhall be pardoned, if with
anticipation I anfwer to fuch a charge.

If to believe that the *French* are engaged in
a juft war—that their fuccefs in it will be favo-
rable to the intereﬅs of liberty—that they are
as brave, generous, and humane a people as any
we know—and to wifh that there may be a
perpetual and moﬅ intimate friendfhip between
them and thefe ﬅates, is to be prejudiced—I
am prejudiced.

If to wifh that *Charles Fox* * may be the
minifter in *Great-Britain*, and that fhe may ne-

---

* *This man's character, with fome fpots, as it
is faid, and not fmall ones upon it, is moﬅ refplen-
dent. For comprehenfion of mind, felection of
points, feizure of opportunities, grandeur of de-
fign, and generofity of thought, he is fo far elevated above his opponents, that their inferiority
muﬅ be manifﬅ to any difpaffionate obferver. Well
might a great hiﬅorian fay of him that—" He was*

ver be conquered by *France*—that fhe may immediately, without lofing an inftant—a perpetuity of confequences may be involved in an
inftant—make peace with her, on terms mutually advantageous—that then they may enjoy a
participation of benefits, enhanced by the participation—and that imitating THE BEING to
whom they owe their happinefs, they may
communicate it as fully as the utmoft exertions
of their united powers will enable them, to
others—fo that the bleffings flowing from their
concord, may far, far exceed " in meafure,
number, and weight," the evils that have
fprung from their difcord, and that amidft the
joy-born acclamations of grateful nations, they
may have an inheritance in the higheft human
felicity, is to be an enemy to *Great-Britain*———
I am her enemy.

---

*a man of honor"—and that—" In the conduct of
a party, he approved himfelf competent to the conduct of an Empire."* Happy *would it have been
for* Britain, *happy for millions, and among them
for the royal family in* France, *if this enlightened
and benevolent ftatefman had prefided over the affairs of his country for the laft feven years.*

*In eloquence he may have equals, but what equals
has he in excellencies of heart?*

In his tour of Switzerland, September, 1788,
*fays the hiftorian in another place, " he gave me
two days of free and private fociety. He feemed
to feel, and even to envy the happinefs of my fituation; while I admired the powers of a fuperior
man, as they are blended in his attractive charac-*

What real *American* can defire the defolation of that land, the birth place of heroes, patriots, fages, and faints—from which we have derived the blood that circulates in our arteries and veins—from which we have received the very current of our thoughts—a land, whofe meads, hills, and ftreams point out the fpots, where her gallant fons met death, face to face, for—LIBERTY : a land, whofe kind-hearted nobles, in every charter wrenched in atteftation of their freedom from the gripe of tyranny, inferted claufes in favor of the commons, while the nobles of other countries, after involving the people in their felfifh quarrels, pretended to be leagues for public good, left them naked to injuries, and made fplendid bargains with

---

ter, with the foftnefs and fimplicity of a child. Perhaps no human being was ever more perfectly exempt from malevolence , vanity, or falfehood."

What an eulogium, from fo able a judge of mankind, and one who difapproved his politics at that time.

If to this knowledge of the man, we add the emphatic import of the memorable words he ufed in parliament, the beginning of laft year, probably all impartial perfons will unite in fentiment upon his merits : they were thefe——" I regard it as a circumftance of good fortune to me that——I NEVER GAVE AN OPINION, BY WHICH ONE DROP OF BRITISH BLOOD WAS SHED, OR ANY OF ITS TREASURES SQUANDERED.

their monarchs for themselves. The after-reckoning foon followed. Their provoked kings broke in upon them. In difmay, they cried out for help, but experienced the holy power of that eternal truth, that—THEY WHO ARE FALSE TO OTHERS, ARE FALSE TO THEMSELVES. There was no help.

To this difference of behaviour, the nobles of *Britain* at this day, in a great meafure owe that portion of freedom in which they partake with the people, when the nobles of other countries are—what I wifh to forget. (So MUCH WISER AND BETTER IS IT TO COM-MUNICATE THAN TO MONOPOLIZE THOSE THINGS, IN WHICH ALL OUGHT TO SHARE.

Another praife is due to *Britain*—for the purity of her tribunals, in the adminiftration of juftice.

The hiftory of mankind, as far as I am acquainted with it, does not afford an inftance, where the ftream has flowed fo clear, for fuch a length of time. Power or faction has not been able to pollute it. The poor and the rich, the labourer and the nobleman, have equal rights to the wholefome draughts. There, even peers are blamelefs.

Yet three evils have fprung up on its fides. One—the labyrinth * of roads leading towards

---

* " *Res admonet, ut de principiis juris, et quibis modis ad* hanc multitudinem infinitam ac varietatem legum *perventumeft, &c.*"

Tac. Ann. Book 3.

R

it : another—the expences of approaching it. The laſt is, that ſome of the agents whoſe duty it has been to facilitate the acceſs, have for their own profit put up falſe directions for thoſe who ſeek it. Theſe evils muſt be removed. To know their title, to ſee but not to taſte the refreſhing waters, is too hard a lot for innocence and diſtreſs.

F A B I U S.

LETTER IX.

MY intention is, to prefent to my countrymen a comparifon between the *Romans* and the *French* on one hand, and between the *Carthaginians* and the *Britifh* on the other; and that then with fuch reflections as may be fuggefted to them, by the information their feveral opportunities may enable them to obtain on fubjects of this fort, they may give themfelves all the fatisfaction that can be acquired from the probabilities of contingency in human affairs, what will be the final event of the war between *France* and *Great-Britain*.

I have not the leaft doubt in my mind, what the event will be : but, this is only the opinion of an individual, fenfible that no weight can be attached to his opinion, unlefs it be fupported by juft reafoning. Whether it is fo fupported, is fubmitted to the confideration of his fellow-citizens.

Different things admit and require different kinds of proof. We do not fee founds or hear light. Things in themfelves may be equally true, and yet to us not be capable of the fame *kind* or *degree* of evidence. From the mifty regions of poffibility, we rife through the pleafing grades of probability, till we arrive at *moral certainty*, its higheft cheerful point: To demand another *kind* or a greater *degree* of evidence than the cafe allows, is to *deceive* ourfelves. It weakens, and with a particular difpofition deftroys the force of that evidence.

which we really have. One error leads to others; and *this temper*, if indulged, will conduct us into abfurdity, contempt of verity, and a fatal rafhnefs. We may think ourfelves at liberty, to determine againft propofitions fup-ported by ftrong evidence, without any evidence equally or nearly as ftrong to juftify that determination. *Hence the* WISDOM *of* INFIDE-LITY. But, we *are not* at liberty to decide, with this imperious peevifhnefs. *Reafon* forbids it; and the conftitution of our nature enforces the prohibition, by its accompanying fanctions. If we were to act thus in the common affairs of life, we fhould become not only ridiculous, but unhappy too: and if we act thus in great affairs, we fhall become more ridiculous and unhappy.

Some eminent geniufes, peremptorily decide againft *propofitions*, though fupported by the beft evidence things of that fort will admit, and for which, fuppofing them to be true, better could not be given. With *them*, nothing is to be affented to or believed, but what has the higheft evidence. All other things are uncertain, loft in a *terra incognita*, unworthy a place among the tenets of the initiated, and fit only for the dull credulity of the profane vulgar. For *their* minds, inflamed with a luft of truth —"DIRA CUPIDO"—*indubitable* certainty will not do. Their afpiring and comprehenfive fouls muft embrace *infallible* certainty.

Yet, in the uniform tenor of their conduct, thefe *Ixions* willingly defcend from their beloved clouds, humbly fubmit to put themfelves upon a level with inferior minds, and meekly condefcend to *be governed*, as they are by *probability:* fo that *reafon* is a very good thing when it accords with their *inclinations*, and a very poor one when it does not. It is therefore very difficult to know, what better faculty than reafon they fuppofe they could have infufed into man, if they had pre-exifted, and been confulted at his creation. In all probability, it would have been brilliant—and ufelefs.

If the ftate of affairs and the courfe of events in our days, appear to concur in announcing a certain cataftrophe, and the experience of mankind in paft ages, under refembling circumftances, teftifies to us, that we ought to expect it, to reject fuch evidence *will be* madnefs, and *may be* deftruction. We have no right to afk, and no reafon to look for—miracles.

What were the *Romans* when they entered into their controverfy with the *Carthaginians*, in comparifon with the *French* at this time? Vaftly—if I did not efteem the word confecrated, I fhould perhaps have faid, *infinitely*—inferior.

The *French* have not yet been again and again, and again, and again, and again, " with the bofom of deftruction," fwept off the feas. They have *fome* knowledge of naval affairs ; *fome* fhips on the ocean, *fome* in the *Mediterranean*, and they have materials for building *fome* more. They have *fome* fhips of *Spain*, and *fome* of *The United Provinces*, to ftrengthen their fleets and fquadrons. They have given *fome* blows in all the four quarters of the world, and are very vigoroufly preparing to give *fome* more.

The future ones will probably be more direct and piercing. From their whole management against their enemies it appears, that they have adopted the maxim of an experienced general of antiquity—" *Strike at the head.*" The application has been as fuccefsful with them as it was formerly. The inftances need not be mentioned.

Great-Britain ftrikes at the nails of *France.* What has fhe got by it? Some hogfheads of fugar. What more? Some bags of coffee. What has fhe loft? Millions of money, and myriads of men—brave men—generous men—loyal men—true men— ——a bad bargain.

The farce of *Corfica* is ended. *Toulon,* one of the ftrongeft harbours known, fome how or other the *Britifh* got. Keep it they could not, any how. Their " *protection*" is perdition; Witnefs its inhabitants and the coafts of *France.* Their " *alliance*" is convulfion. Witnefs *The United provinces.* What their " *refpect*" is, the ftates of *Italy,* and fome other ftates, can tell. Their fleets have been fo triumphant, that moft of the ports in *Europe* are fhut againft their commerce. More, it is likely, will be fhut. *Ours,* indeed, are open to them. I acknowledge the greatnefs of this advantage.

Some other of their acquifitions ought to be mentioned. They have feized *The Cape of Good Hope,* parts of *Ceylon,* and the *Molucca iflands.*

Of what importance are thefe places, as to THE SUM OF THE WAR? Abfolutely of none. They are worfe. They will weaken their efforts at home and near home. If they were to make more fuch acquifitions, it would be ftill worfe. They may go on victorioufly in this way, till they conquer themfelves—into deftruction; and the fucceffors of the ancient *Gauls* may well laugh, as I doubt not they do, to fee their rough predeceffor's maxim fo whimfically reverfed, from " *Væ victis*," to " *Væ victoribus*."

One ftrong grafp on *Ireland*, or any county in *Britain*, will obtain a reftoration of all her acquifitions—AND MORE.

Will the *French* never make fuch a grafp? If the war continues a little longer, moft certainly they will. They have hitherto been employed in clearing their way to the bofom of *Britain*. I dread the blows that will be ftruck *there*. Can *Britifh* fkill, great as it is, command the winds? Can *Britifh* valor, diftinguifhed at it is, act where it is not? How often have their fleets been locked up for weeks together by gales, at the fame time fair for the operations of enemies if determined on a defcent? From *Breft* to *The Dollart Sea*, the whole confronting coafts are hoftile, with a variety of inflections exceedingly favourable to invafion of the oppofite fhores. *England* had a very ftrong fleet, when invaded by *William* the firft; and alfo when invaded by *William* the third.*

---

* * In the year 287, Caraufius *affumed in* Britain, *the imperial purple and title of* Auguftus. *He extended his power over a great part of* Gaul, *and reigned feven years. He was fucceeded by* Allectus. *The emperor* Conftantius *determined to attempt*

Befides, the *French* entertain a livelier refentment againft *Great-Britain*, than againft any of her enemies. Their exertions againft her will therefore be *more* intenfe, if poffible, than they have been againft their other enemies. If they fhould be fo, the word *more* juft now ufed, will be found to denote fomething greater than an ILIAD.

" *Et* dubitemus *ad huc* virtute *extendere* vires *?*
                                    Virgil.

And *doubt* we yet by *virtuous* acts to rife,
When fame, when fafety is the mighty
        prize?
RISE! RISE! my brethren! *Punic* foes
        o'ercome—
RISE! the " *lov'd allies*" of majeftic ROME.

                        FABIUS.

---

the recovery *of* Britain. *The weather was favourable to the enterprize.* " *The* ROMANS, *under the cover of a thick fog,* efcaped *the fleet of* Allectus ; *and* convinced *the* BRITONS, *that a* fuperiority of naval ftrength will not always protect their country from a foreign invafion."
        Gibb. *Hift.* 2. 106.

LETTER X.

A Confideration of high importance claims our moft fixed attention—the TEMPER of the *French*.

The great hiftorian who has been quoted, was an eminent philofopher and ftatefman. He had the beft opportunities for acquiring knowledge, by living in times of the greateft action, and in habits of intimacy with the moft diftinguifhed actors.

In the fecond *Punic* war, the '' *dire Hanibal*'' was at laft expelled from *Italy*, and in the fields of *Zama* the doom of the world was determined.

In the third war, *Carthage* perifhed to the roots.*

When *Scipio Africanus* the younger entered the principal ftreet of the devoted city, then taken, and in flames, he held *Polybius* by the hand. The fhort converfation between them, it could not but be fhort, was pathetic in the extreme; and therefore, I hope, every reader of fenfibility will excufe a recital of it.

As they advanced among the blazing houfes, and the flying, falling citizens, *Scipio* with emotion repeated fome lines of *Homer* defcribing *Troy* in the fame circumftances they now faw *Carthage*——

---

* '' Carthago, *æmula imperii* Romani, *a ftirpe periit*.''   Sall.

S

" Yet—come it will, the day decreed by
    fates,
" How my heart trembles while my tongue
    relates !
" The day when thou, imperial TROY, shall
    bend,
" And see thy warriors fall, thy glories
    end——"*

Polybius asked the general why he repeated
those lines in so tender a manner, in the midst

---

* [The remainder of this speech of Hector to
Andromache, consists of those lines :—
" And yet no dire presage so wounds my mind,
" My mother's death, the ruin of my kind,
" Not Priam's hoary hairs defiled with gore,
" Not all my brothers gasping on the shore ;
" As thine, Andromache ! thy griefs I dread :
" I see thee trembling, weeping, captive led !
" In Argive looms our battles to design,
" And woes, of which so large a part was thine !
" To bear the victor's hard commands, or bring
" The weight of waters from Hyperia's spring.
" There, while you groan beneath the load of life,
" They cry—Behold the mighty Hector's wife !
" Some haughty Greek, who lives thy tears to see,
" Imbitters all thy woes, by naming me.
" The thoughts of glory past, and present shame,
" A thousand griefs shall waken at the name.
" May I lie cold before that dreadful day,
" Press'd with a load of monumental clay !
" Thy Hector, wrapt in everlasting sleep,
" Shall neither hear thee sigh, nor see thee weep.'

of his fuccefs againft enemies? *Scipio* anfwered, that in viewing the deftruction of *Carthage*, he contemplated the uncertainty of empire, with a foreboding apprehenfion, that the moft profperous, might fome time or other fhare the fame fate.

The hiftorian being a man of bufinefs, and well acquainted with the world, his obfervations are drawn from life and manners, and therefore the fragments of his work are held in fuch univerfal efteem.

He tells us, that "THE ROMANS PREVAILED BY A CERTAIN INFLEXIBILITY PECULIAR TO THEMSELVES."

Have not the *French* fufficiently fhewn, that they have an equal "INFLEXIBILITY?" That of the *Romans* appears to have been at times relaxed. When has that of the *French* ever been relaxed? Difficulties, diftreffes, defeats, varied, complicated, calling on all fides for remedy or relief, they have met with. There have been paufes in their affairs, of prognofticating continuance. What followed? Vollies of victories. Battles loft have been preludes to battles won. Retreats have been waited on by conquefts. Mountains, fortifications, rivers fluent or frozen, the heats of fummer, the frofts of winter, have not damped their fpirits or ftopped their career. There is a fpring in their minds, to which weight gives energy. Their caufe animates them with inextinguifhable excitement. They are fighting for FREEDOM, and are fully perfuaded, that they muft crufh their enemies, to fecure it. The bufinefs comes home to the heart. The public caufe is every man's own caufe.

" And each contends as his were all the war."

What a *temper* is this! that, move it any way, has the fteadinefs of a cube—prefs it any way, has the elafticity of air.

If their *perfeverance* waited twelve months for *a fingle object*, impregnable *Luxemburgh*, which they obtained: and again has waited nearly as long for another, almoft unapproachable *Mantua*, now probably in their hands too, what will not they venture, what will not they fuffer, for the province of *Munfter*, or the county of *Cornwall*, either of them the firft ftep to ————————

Their *enterprize* is equal to their perfeverance. What other nation ever formed, and fo far executed, a plan for the excifion of a vaft *maritime* commerce, fcarcely vulnerable on water, by conquering round the coafts of the feas on which it is managed.

In fhort, there is no other ftop to their efforts, than the entire accomplifhment of their defigns —for they

" Think nothing *done*, while aught remains to *do*."

FABIUS.

LETTER XI.

SOME years, some little years ago, there were such things as *gratitude* and *friendship* between nations, believed in by the people of these States, and with a fervor of conviction, in ardor and assurance inferior only to a good man's religious faith, or———they were all *liars*.

They were not *liars*. They uttered what they thought. Their tongues were the interpreters of their souls. He who never erred has told us, that " of the abundance of the heart the mouth speaketh," and surely there was an "*abundance*," for our mouths to speak from.

How uncertain, at least how remote, must have been the issue of our war with *Great-Britain*——what an accumulation of distresses upon those we were enduring, must we have suffered, if it had not been for the aids we received from *France?* Let us endeavour as well as we can, to recollect what we have seen, heard, and felt, and to convey our experience to our children.

How did the nation *most solemnly* express their sentiments by their Representatives in Congress ?

" The treaties between his most Christian majesty and *The United States of America*, so fully demonstrate his wisdom and magnanimity, as to command *the reverence of all nations*. The VIRTUOUS citizens of *America* CAN NEVER FORGET his beneficent attention to their violated rights, NOR CEASE TO ACKNOWLEDGE

THE HAND OF A GRACIOUS PROVIDENCE in raifing them up fo powerful and illuftrious a FRIEND.

—" *This affembly are convinced*—that had it refted folely with the moft Chriftian King, not only the *independence* of thefe ftates would have been univerfally acknowledged, but their *tranquility* fully eftablifhed"—" We ardently wifh to fheathe the fword, and *fpare the further effufion of blood*"—Congrefs have reafon to believe, that THE ASSISTANCE SO WISELY AND GENEROUSLY SENT WILL BRING *Great-Britain* to a fenfe of juftice and moderation, *promote* the *interefts of France and America*, and *fecure peace and tranquility*, on the moft firm and honourable foundation. Neither can it be doubted, that thofe who adminifter the powers of government, within the feveral ftates of this union, will *cement that connection with* THE SUBJECTS OF FRANCE, the beneficent effects of which have already been fo fenfibly felt.*

" You have conducted the great military conteft with wifdom and fortitude, invariably regarding the rights of the civil power through all difafters and changes ; you have by the love and confidence of your fellow-citizens, enabled them to difplay their martial genius, and tranfmit their fame to pofterity : you have perfevered till thefe United States, AIDED BY A MAGNANIMOUS KING AND NATION,

---

* *Journals of Congrefs*, Auguft 6*th*, 1778.

have been enabled, UNDER A JUST PRO-
VIDENCE, to clofe the war in *freedom, fafety,*
and *independence.**

" If other motives than that of *juftice* could
be requifite on this occafion, NO NATION
COULD EVER FEEL STRONGER ; for
to *whom* are the debts to be paid ?

" To AN ALLY, in the firft place, who to
THE EXERTION OF HIS ARMS in fup-
port of our caufe, has added THE SUC-
COURS OF HIS TREASURES, who to his
IMPORTANT LOANS has added LIBERAL
DONATIONS ; and *whofe loans themfelves carry
the imprcffion of his magnanimity* " *and* FRIEND-
SHIP."—

" If juftice, good faith, honour, *gratitude,*
and all the other qualities which ennoble *the
charaƈter of a nation,* and fulfil the ends of government, be the fruits of our eftablifhments,
the caufe of liberty will acquire a dignity and
luftre which it has never yet enjoyed ; and an
example will be fet which cannot but have the
moft favourable influence on the rights of mankind. If, on the other fide, our government
fhould be UNFORTUNATELY blotted with
the reverfe of thefe *cardinal* and *effential* VIR-
TUES, the *great caufe* which we have engaged to
vindicate, *will be difhonored and betrayed* ; the *laft*
and *faireft* experiment IN FAVOR OF THE
RIGHTS OF HUMAN NATURE, *will be*

* *Journals of Congrefs*, Dec. 23d, 1783.

turned againſt them, and THEIR PATRONS AND FRIENDS, expoſed to be INSULTED and ſilenced by *the votaries of tyranny and uſurpation.*"*

How baſe ſpirited, how contemptible muſt our Repreſentatives in Congreſs have been, had they not expreſſed ſuch ſentiments with reſpect to THE FRENCH NATION AND THEIR CHIEF MAGISTRATE, as they did?

They *knew*, that his conduct towards us *deſerved* " THE REVERENCE OF ALL NATIONS," their well choſen phraſe; for the ſincerity, good-nature, liberality, generoſity, and magnanimity therein diſplayed, ſtand, I believe, unequalled in any inſtance of negociation which the ample repoſitories of diplomatic literature can furniſh.

Truth has been cunningly diſguiſed by a laboured compilation, intended to deceive and irritate the citizens of theſe ſtates, as if a meritorious vigilance had been happily exerted to explore in a number of political tranſactions, the baſe and artful motives that lay lurking, under a pretended friendſhip on his part towards theſe ſtates.

The real fact is, that at the very beginning of our acquaintance with him, which he ſo diligently cultivated till it ripened into a friendſhip bearing a profuſion of the richeſt fruits, he came forward boldly, like an HONEST MAN, and TOLD US PLAINLY, that *the intereſt* of *France*, as well as of theſe ſtates, induced him to enter into an alliance with us.

* *Journals of Congreſs*, April 26th, 1783.

" On the 16th day of December, 1777, the commiffioners of Congrefs were informed by Mr. *Girard*, one of the fecretaries of the King's Council of State, that it was decided to acknowledge the independence of *The United States*, and to make a treaty with them. That in the treaty *no advantage would be taken of* their fituation to obtain terms which otherwife, it would not be convenient for them to agree to. That His Moft Chriftian Majefty defired the treaty once made fhould be *durable*, and THEIR AMITY TO CONTINUE FOR EVER, which could not be expected if EACH NATION *did not find an intereft in its continuance*, as well as in its commencement. It was therefore intended, that the terms of the treaty fhould be fuch as *the new formed States* would be willing to agree to if they had been long fince eftablifhed, and *in the fulnefs of ftrength and power;* and fuch as they fhould approve of when that time fhould come. That His Moft Chriftian Majefty was fixed in his determination not only to *acknowledge*, but to *fupport* their *independence*. That in doing this he might probably foon *be engaged in a war*, yet HE SHOULD NOT EXPECT ANY COMPENSATION from the United States on that account. NOR WAS IT PRETENDED THAT HE ACTED WHOLLY FOR THEIR SAKES; fince befides his real good will to them, IT WAS MANIFESTLY THE INTEREST OF FRANCE, that the power of *England* fhould be diminifhed by the feparation of the colonies from its government. That the *only condition* he fhould require and rely on would be, that

T

The United States in no peace to be made, fhould give up their *independence*, and return to the obedience of the *Britifh* government."*

On the thirtieth day of *January*, 1778, the king appointed and commiffioned the Sieur *Girard* his plenipotentiary, and on the fixth day of the next month, the treaties of alliance and of amity and commerce were figned.

On the fixth day of *Auguft*, 1778, the Sieur *Girard* was introduced to an audience and delivered to the prefident of congrefs a letter from His Moft Chriftian Majefty, directed,

" To our very dear great friends and allies, the prefident and members of the general congrefs of *The United States* of *North America*:

" Very dear friends and great allies : The treaties which we have figned with you, *in confequence of the propofals your commiffioners made to us in your behalf*, are a certain affurance of our affection for *The United States* in general, and for each of them in particular, as well as the intereft *we take and conftantly fhall take* in their happinefs and profperity. It is to convince you more particularly of this, that we have nominated the Sieur *Girard*, fecretary of our council of ftate, to refide among you in quality of minifter plenipotentiary. He is the better acquainted with our fentiments towards you, and the more capable of teftifying the fame to you, as he was entrufted on our part to negociate with

* *The Hiftory of the American Revolution, vol.* II. *page* 63, *by* David Ramfay, M. D. *the Polybius of* America.

your commiffioners, and figned with them *the treaties which cement our union.* I pray you will give all credit to all he fhall communicate to you from us, more efpecially when he fhall affure you of our affection and conftant friendfhip for you. We pray GOD, very dear great friends, to have you in his holy keeping.

Your good friend and ally,

LOUIS.

Verfailles, the 28th of *March,* 1778.
    Gravier de Vergennes."

The minifter was then announced to the houfe : whereupon he arofe and addreffed congrefs in a fpeech, which when he had finifhed, his fecretary delivered in writing to the prefident, and is as follows :

  " Gentlemen,

" The connection formed by the king my mafter, with *The United States of America,* is fo agreeable to him, that he could no longer delay fending me to refide among you, for the purpofe of cementing it. It will give his majefty great fatisfaction to learn, that the *fentiments which have fhone forth on this occafion,* juftify that confidence with which he hath been infpired by the zeal and character of the commiffioners of *The United States* in *France,* the wifdom and fortitude which have directed the refolutions of congrefs, and the courage and perfeverance of the people they reprefent ; a confidence which you know, gentlemen, has been the bafis of *that amicable and truly difinterefted fyftem,* on which he had treated with *The United States.*

T 2

" It is not his majesty's fault, that the engagements he hath entered into did not establish
your independence and repose, without the further
effusion of blood, and without aggravating the
calamities of mankind, whose happiness it is
his highest ambition to promote and secure,
but since the hostile measures and designs of the
common enemy have given to engagements,
purely eventual, an immediate, positive, permanent, and indissoluble force, it is the opinion of the king my master, that the allies
should turn their whole attention to fulfil those
engagements in the manner most useful to the
common cause, and best calculated to obtain
that peace which is the object of the alliance.
It is upon this principle, gentlemen, that his
majesty has hastened to send you a *powerful
assistance*, which you owe only to his friendship,
to the sincere regard he has for every thing
which relates to the advantage of *The United
States*, and *the desire of contributing* WITH EF-
FICACY *to establish your repose and prosperity
upon an honorable and solid foundation*: And further, it is his expectation, that the principles
which may be adopted by the respective governments will tend to strengthen those bonds
of union, which have originated in THE MU-
TUAL INTEREST OF THE TWO NATIONS.
The principal object of my instructions is, *to
cement the interests of France with those of the
United States.*

" I flatter myself, gentlemen, that my past
conduct in the affairs which concern them, hath
already convinced you of the determination I

feel, to endeavour to obey my inftructions in fuch manner, as to deferve the confidence of congrefs, the friendfhip of its members, and the efteem of the citizens of *America.*"

(Signed)

GIRARD.

To which the prefident returned the following anfwer:

SIR,

The treaties between his moft Chriftian majefty and *The United States of America*, fo fully demonftrate his wifdom and magnanimity, *as to command the reverence of all nations.* The *virtuous* citizens of *America* in particular, *can never forget* his beneficent attention to their violated rights, *nor ceafe to acknowledge the hand of* A GRACIOUS PROVIDENCE *in raifing them up fo powerful and illuftrious* A FRIEND. It is the hope and opinion of congrefs, that the confidence his majefty repofes in the firmnefs of thefe ftates, will receive additional ftrength from every day's experience.

This affembly are convinced, fir, that had it refted folely with the moft Chriftian king, *not only the independence* of thefe ftates would have been *univerfally acknowledged,* but their *tranquility eftablifhed.* We lament that luft of domination which gave birth to the prefent war, and hath prolonged and extended the miferies of mankind. We ardently wifh to fheathe the fword, and *fpare the further effufion of human blood;* but we are determined by every means in our power, to fulfil thofe eventual engagements which have acquired pofitive and permanent force from the hoftile defigns and meafures of the common enemy.

Congrefs have reafon to believe, that the affiftance fo wifely and generoufly fent WILL BRING *Great-Britain* to a fenfe of juftice and moderation, *promote the interefts of France and America,* and *fecure peace and tranquility on the moft firm and honourable foundations.* Neither can it be doubted that thofe who adminifter the powers of government, within the feveral ftates of this union, will cement that *connection with the fubjects of France, the beneficial effects of which have been already fo effentially felt.*

SIR,

From the experience we have had of your exertions to PROMOTE THE TRUE INTERESTS OF OUR COUNTRY AS WELL AS YOUR OWN, it is with the higheft fatisfaction congrefs receives as the firft minifter from his moft Chriftian majefty, a gentleman whofe paft conduct affords a happy prefage, that he merits the confidence of this body, the friendfhip of its members, and the efteem of the citizens of *America.*

FABIUS.

LETTER XII.

FRENCHMEN fought, bled, and died for us.

"So they did," it is faid, "but their monarch bade them fight, bleed, and die for us, and they were obliged to do fo, and all our gratitude and friendfhip, if there was any gratitude or friendfhip in the cafe, was due to him alone."

Generous diftinction! We are to have no confideration whatever for thofe men, nor for their pofterity, nor for their country, becaufe they performed what *they* thought to be *their* duty, and what *we* felt and ftill feel to be *our* happinefs.

How far was our gratitude or friendfhip to carry us? Did it extend to *the heirs of the king?* "Yes, if there was any due to him; becaufe *he* was our benefactor." Futile evafion! Too pretending, to have any honeft meaning! Why not then to *his people?* Ought *they* not to have been as dear to *him*, ought they not to be as dear to *us* as his children? *He* was a *Frenchman*—and under the fupreme fovereignty of infinite goodnefs, wifdom, and power, in his tranfactions with us, the *conftitutional* agent for and reprefentative of all the people of *France*. He was known *to us*, he was connected *with us*, as the *ruler of that people*, not as *the father of children*. What was he without them? They gave him his power, his abilities and inclinations to aid us, *were all*

French His abilities, it is evident to the haftieft obfervation, were fo. His inclinations too, were all *French*; not merely as the inclination of an individual or *part* of that nation: but, becaufe they arofe from that combination of circumftances, that actuating complexity of thoughts, manners, cuftoms, and ftate of things, whofe focial operation pervaded the nation, and in which he by the laws of nature partook.

His counfellors were *Frenchmen.* Thofe who were continually about him, were *Frenchmen.* He was not a folitary being eftranged from all the influences of fuch a fituation. No! We have had affecting proofs, that he was a man of fenfibility, found fenfe, and much ufeful information.*

The *French* loved liberty, when they did not enjoy it. They never forgot, that their anceftors were free, and were cheated out of their freedom; or that their very *name* attefted their imprefcriptible rights. Unhappy *Louis!* to perifh at their renovation.

---

* *Volumes have been written to ftigmatize the character of the late king and queen of France.— The charges, tho' formally made, have not been proved: and when we confider, with what art, and with what defigns fo many fcandalous reports were propagated againft* Louis *the XVI. and his confort—and who were the perfons moft induftrious, and moft interefted as they fuppofed, in the effects expected to be derived from the unpopularity of the* King *and* Queen, *there is no reafon for our believing, that truth has been regarded in thefe reproaches. The infamy of accufers, is a vindication.*

"We cannot recal him from the impaffable bourn of his abode, to rejoice with his country in their profperity, or to render us any further kindneffes: but, fuppofing him living, dethroned, and permitted to addrefs thefe States, have we not reafon to believe, that fomething like this would be his language?

" *Very great dear friends,*

In the courfe of events, over which Divine Providence prefides, I no longer govern the *French.* The fovereignty is exercifed immediately by themfelves. The form of government is changed. *The nation is the fame.* They are the people FOR WHOSE BENEFIT, as I CANDIDLY informed you, I entered into treaties with you, of alliance, and of amity and commerce. A purfuit of *their* happinefs juftified me to myfelf, in expofing them to the evils of war, and left me at liberty to gratify " my real good will" to you.

I was perfuaded, that our united efforts would bring the war to fuch a termination, as would compenfate for its evils, and that a perfect amity between the two allied nations, would be productive of diftinguifhed bleffings to both of them.

We fucceeded.

If you think, that the affiftance you received from *France, enabled you to clofe the war on an honorable and firm foundation, in freedom, fafety, and independence,"** and if on that account you regard me with fentiments of *gratitude* and *friendfhip,* as I am convinced by your warm

---

* *Expreffions ufed by Congrefs.*

V

and repeated declarations you do, I cannot
doubt your compliance with the last request I
shall ever make to you, dictated as it is in a
great degree, by my unabated esteem for you,
an inclination of which the indulgence has always brought me the sincerest pleasure.

My request is, that you may wholly tranf-
fer from me a citizen of *France* to that people
who empowered me to render you essential fer-
vices, all the sentiments of gratitude and friendfhip which you feel for me. Those sentiments
have been attached to my person, by the station
I held from them, a station at the most according to the laws of nature but of short duration,
by their distresses, by their treasures, and by
their blood. *Place the sentiments where they are
most justly due.* If you love me, love those
whom I love, and *for whose " sake"* I first loved
you. *That will be the best evidence you can give
of your affection for me.*

As weighty considerations as prompted the
alliance, recommend its continuance. It is as
manifest to me now, as it was at the beginning
of our correspondence, that the reciprocation
of benefits will be incomputable, increasing,
and never can be obstructed, unless one party
should seek to advance itself at the expence of
the other, which is not to be expected."

If these were the sentiments of this good
prince towards the conclusion of his life, how
much was he deceived?

It was his doom to live, not only in an age
of revolutions in government, but also of revolutions in morality.

Scarcely was his head laid low in the duft, probably in confequence of our liberty being eftablifhed, fcarcely were thofe lips clofed in eternal filence, which never fpoke to us but in the language of benediction, fcarcely was that exiftence, to which, after virtue and piety fair fame was deareft, diffolved, and difabled to vindicate an afperfed reputation, than———a fevere fcrutiny was made into his unfceptered merits, and it was difcovered———by *Americans* ———Yes———by *Americans*———that *he himfelf* was not entitled to *our* gratitude or friendfhip, but was a felfifh unprincipled villain.

Much injured LOUIS!

The charges of thy accufers *undefignedly* erect a lafting monument to thy glory. They have proved thee guilty———of fincerely loving thy people. Thy feet were led into unbeaten, un-explored tracts of policy, and thou hadft not been accuftomed to its intricate mazes. Im-pelled by thy benevolence towards us, a young, innocent, oppreffed, and unexperienced peo-ple, ftruggling in blood, and hardly able to ftruggle, though the prize was no lefs than PEACE, LIBERTY AND SAFETY, againft the then moft formidable nation in the world, and by thy tender affection for *France* recently weakened by deep wounds received from the fame enemy, thou formedft the kind and gene-rous refolution to help us AT OUR UTMOST NEED, though the execution of thy noble de-fign would exhibit to mankind, the furprizing fpectacle of—a *Republic* foftered by a *Monarchy* —and in a portion of the globe far remote from thy kingdom—and in the neighbourhood of thy moſt valuable foreign dominions——And thou didſt help us "*effeⅽtually*" till every man among us " from one end of our land to the other, and from one ſide of our land to the other," "DWELT CONFIDENTLY," with his family, " under his vine and under his fruit tree," and ALLIED with thee and thy people, there was "NONE TO MAKE US AFRAID."

But, in directing the courſe of thy exertions through an unknown wildernefs, dangers might ſtart up on every ſide. Thy accuſers have convicted thee, of being more anxious for the welfare of thy people, than for that of ſtrangers—Yet—Heaven and earth are witneſſes, that to thee, to thee, under " *a gracious Providence which raiſed thee up to be our friend,*"* " *We the people of the United States*" ſtand indebted for the beſt of bleſſings—*Liberty.*

" Manibus date *Lilia* plenis :
" Purpureos ſpargam, ſtores, animamque" *Amici*
" His ſaltem adcumulem donis, et fungar inani
" Munere———

BringLILIES—LILIESin wholehandfulsbring
With all the purple fragrance of the ſpring ;
Theſe unavailing gifts let me beſtow :
'Tis all I can—on thy dear ſhade below.—

F A B I U S.

* *Words of Congreſs.*

LETTER XIII.

IT is afferted among us, that no *gratitude* is due to men, and there is no *friendſhip* in them for us, if in their conduct towards us however *kind* and *beneficial*, they are influenced by a regard for their own interefts.

This propofition demands our attention, efpecially as it is induſtrioufly propagated, in order to produce a revulfion of the public fentiment from particular objects, which we have been accuſtomed to view in another light, and that revulfion is intended to bring on confequences, in which the welfare of thefe ftates muft be deeply concerned.

In the conftitution which our maker has affigned to man, two difpofitions are obfervable; *love of felf*, and *focial affection*. They are compatible, innocently, virtuoufly, advantageoufly compatible, or they would not have been " joined together." Their union is the means to good ends.

It is not neceffary here to controvert the opinion of a celebrated author, that no ideas are innate, though he argues with a weaknefs exceedingly furprifing in fo great a man, when he embarraffes queftions refpecting a *general faculty* by deductions from *particular incapacities*, a fcheme as indefenfible as his frame of government for *Carolina*.*

* *The famous* Grecian *philofopher was more accurate when he diftinguiſhed between the qualities of capacity and completion.*

It is fufficient if there are *natural propenfities* *
in man to good. Thefe may perhaps not improperly be called *the feeds* of good. But as
the planted feeds of vegetables, require funfhine, air, rain, and cultivation, to bring them
to the perfection of which they are capable, fo
the feeds in the mind require, if the expreffion
is allowable, funfhine, air, rain, and cultivation, fuitable for bringing *them* to the perfection
of which *they* are capable. Thus it is as to
reafon, an undifputed faculty of human nature,
though all individuals do not partake of it ; and
in thofe who do, what gradations ! from a
Tongutfian, fcraping his fcanty utenfils and
worfhipping fetiches made of fhreds, to a
Newton, weighing the planets, explaining the

As referring to the human mind, capacity *is*
the faculty of reafoning, *and* completion *is the*
act of reafoning.

It has not been thought requifite to purfue the
elaborate invefligation of thofe who contend, that
self-love *and* focial affection *are not implanted in*
our nature, but are gradually formed in us by com-
munication with others, fince it is evident that
men are fo made and fo placed in creation, that
thefe difpofitions by fixed laws neceffarily and natu-
rally grow up from their make and fituation.

For upon this hypothefis, it is manifeftly the good
pleafure of our Creator, that thefe falutary and
beneficial difpofitions fhould exift in his creatures of
mankind.

* Locke's *Effay on human underflanding.* Book
I. *chap.* iii. § 3. 12. *chap.* iv. § 11.

principles by which the material univerſe is
ſuſtained, and the motion of its ponderous orbs
determined, and proving the exiſtence of Deity,
from the wonders of his works.*

How feeble the outſet of reaſon, how diver-
ſified its progreſs, how almoſt-boundleſs its
advancement! Wing'd by diligence and hope,
it ſprings from earth, awhile ſurveys its pre-
cious objects, then ſoars to the utmoſt verge of
our ſyſtem, there ſums its powers, aſpires into
ſpace, bends its courſe among innumerable
ſuns and worlds, diſcerns *immenſity*, breathes
of *eternity*, and ſtruck into the deepeſt humility, proſtrates itſelf before the footſtool of HIS
throne to WHOM they *both* belong.

This globe of ours therefore is a *ſpeck* in
creation. *Self* is a *ſpeck* upon this globe.

The well - prepared mind riſes through
the ſenſibilities † of kindred, to thoſe

---

* *Letters from* Sir Iſaac Newton *to* Dr. Bentley.

† *Private and* public *affections are ſo reſembling,
that their origin appears to be the ſame.*

Private affections are ſources of happineſs.
*Our own feelings convince us of this delightful
truth. The enjoyment teaches us, to eſtimate and
venerate the like happineſs in* others, *and to deſire
its increaſe. The heart is ſoftened, improved, and
expanded by this exerciſe.* Univerſal benevolence
ſeems to grow naturally from ſuch ſenſations.

*We know not the extent or duration of the hap-
pineſs we may produce, by one act of kindneſs to a
fellow-creature; neither can we compute the miſery
we may cauſe by a ſingle injury. How much ought*

of friendſhip, neighbourhood, acquaintance, and country, all of them related, luminous, and delightful. Untired and unſatisfied it travels on. Other aſſociations *ſtill variouſly recommended*, preſent themſelves. Something is yet wanting: It proceeds. It approaches its deſignated dignity, and at length recognizes its *relation to mankind*, through a COMMON PARENT of infinite perfections, who beholds them all with impartial love. The mind can ſeek no more. Filled with truth, it adores the goodneſs that deſigned this *ſyſtem of affections*, and haſtens to perform the parts allotted to it in the arrangement.

In our attention to this plan, we may perceive, that earthly things move on heavenly principles. Virtue eſſentially and in its nature has a tenden-

---

we to dread the ſlighteſt deviation from our Saviour's *unequalled rule*—"AS YE WOULD THAT MEN SHOULD DO TO YOU, DO YE ALSO TO THEM LIKEWISE.

Private affections *may generate* univerſal benevolence, *and* univerſal benevolence *may advance the happineſs derived from* private affections ; *but, certainly is never in oppoſition to them. It is a* kindred affection *of the great family of love.*

The precepts of the Chriſtian *religion relating to ſocial virtues, are continually employed in the elucidation, eſtabliſhment, recommendation, and enforcement of* THIS MOST IMPORTANT TRUTH.

Plato, *on the contrary, in order to produce general affections, deemed it neceſſary utterly to extinguiſh private affections. His project of bringing up children at the public expence, and never permit-*

cy to produce happiness: Vice on the contrary, essentially and in its nature has a tendency to produce misery. It follows, that all virtue is wisdom, and all vice is folly.

There is therefore in the divine gifts no *hostility* to good. *Evil* proceeds from the neglect or abuse of them. How the neglect or abuse of them in some cases is to be accounted for, is a point not pertinent to the present discussion. Any sincere enquirer after truth may find sufficient reasons,

" To justify the ways of GOD to man."

Neither is there any *discordance* between the divine gifts. But, if men will neglect or abuse them, or if they will attempt with a false philosophy to set them at variance, they must gather such fruits as such a culture of their *reason* yields them.

There is a harmony then in the several DISPOSITIONS which our Creator has given to our nature, and our happiness arises from the combination of these varieties. Each may be indulged not only innocently, but meritoriously. It is not only the right, but the duty of men, to pursue their own happiness. Right involves a duty. They grossly err, if they suppose they can obtain it, by disregarding the happiness of others. *Self love* and *social* are as intimately united as colours in a ray of light.

---

ting them to know their nearest relations, would have been an education of ENEMIES TO THE HUMAN ⅂ CE.

W

The ray without one of them would be imperfect. The due regulation of them, is the perfection of man's character. He may not at
once attain it; but he may, if he will. By
faithful attention, inferior confiderations will
be made to give way to fuperior; and if he is
not a phlegmatic fplitter of a thought or a cold
diffector of a fenfation,* love for himfelf and
others will be fo blended in his mind, that he will
not wifh to feparate them, and perhaps cannot.
When the edifice of moral improvement is thus
far completed, the man becomes as different
from fome others, if not from what he himfelf
once was, as the beft houfes among us are from
the huts of our poor *Indians.*

We have bodies and minds. Our rights and
duties, defires and averfions, affections and
paffions are all true to *us,* if we will but be true
to *them.* Pleafures and pains are held out to us
in this life by the conftitution of our nature, as
motives to right behaviour. Rewards and pu-
nifhments in another life, are alfo held out to
us exprefsly by divine authority, for the fame
purpofe. Here is a double provifion addreffed

---

* *The word* " *Senfation*" *is here ufed in* Mon-
tefquieu's *fenfe.* " *Virtue in a Republic is a* moft
fimple thing; *it is a love for the Republic; it is
a* fenfation, *and not a confequence of acquired knowledge; a* fenfation *that may be felt by the meaneft
as well as by the higheft perfon in the ftate.*"

The love of Friends *and* Benefactors *is a* fenfation. *It is a law of Nature. It is a Com-
mandment from Heaven.*

to our *selfishnefs*. For what? To direct us to virtue and happinefs. Was there any wifdom or goodnefs in thefe directions? Surely. Are we blameable for being guided by them? Certainly not. If refpected as they ought to be, they will gradually form in us a temper of the higheft and brighteft luftre.

We read of our bleffed Saviour in the Scriptures, that "*for the joy that was fet before him, he endured the crofs.*" Dare we deny, that there was merit in his fufferings, becaufe he expected to be rewarded? Or dare we deny, that he was our "*Friend,*" and that we are under obligations to him for them?

Where will this "*new doctrine*" concerning gratitude and friendfhip carry us?

'Tis true, that individuals and nations attend to their own interefts, and fo they ought to do: but it is as true, that they cannot wifely and effectually attend to them, unlefs they attend alfo to thofe of others. Human excellence and happinefs depend on the union of the two difpofitions. Why fhould maxims be introduced among us, a young people, to fhake this falutary truth? Why fhould principles be calculated for checking, and even extirpating from our hearts, thofe very propenfities which our Maker has planted there—benignant and noble propenfities—WITHOUT THE CULTIVATION OF WHICH the world never can reap that harveft of peace and felicity, which it is deftined to enjoy.

It is aftonifhing, that perfons who feem to have a refpect for religion, and therefore may

be prefumed to have a deteftation for the thefes
of fome metaphyfical *ballooners*, fhould feri-
oufly adopt one of the worft articles in their
dreary and chaotic creed, which is—that "men
are governed by a fordid motive, if they are
influenced by a regard for their own interefts:"
for, what is the inference immediately drawn
from the admiffion of this *lemma?* This—
"That the *Chriftian* Religion, in propofing
fuch a motive, is nothing more than a vile contrivance to excite the fears of men, and then to
rule over them by managing their fears."

This *abhorring imitation* is a ftrange jumble;
an unlucky attempt to reconcile a true religion
and a falfe policy.

According to thefe fortunately difcovered
Pandects, all the intercourfes of life are to be
obftructed and embittered, becaufe GOD has
made men to love themfelves.

"Take care of the pernicious difpofition,"
fay the learned expounders—"beware of the
lion covered with a lamb's fleece." All individuals and nations regard their own interefts.
Terrible truth! Sufpect them. As to *fome particulars*, bravely fhew, that you fufpect them
more than you do their enemies. "This conduct may bring on alienation." No matter.
"It may even bring on fomething worfe."
Mind not that. WE NEVER CAN MISTAKE.
Why fhould you be fo unreafonable, as to trouble
yourfelves about your own falvation? None but
*the enemies of "order and good government," of
"morality and religion,"* can be fo headftrong.
Avoid thofe *partizans of confufion:* thofe poli-

tical *enthusiasts*, who are always dreaming of a Heaven of Liberty, when they ought to be working upon the World for Wealth. Abominate the *disorganizers!* Confide in *our cool-blooded regularity.* Our conduct is CONSUMMATE POLICY ; and if you *perish*, you may have the satisfaction of knowing, that you perish, " *secundum artem* : And what an *Euthanasia* must that be ?"

I don't like this " *new doctrine.*" I think we had a better before. I am contented with the volume of nature, the Old Testament and the New Testament. I want no more. These last contain adequate and unparalleled maxims for the conduct of private and public life.

A man meets a stranger on business, who behaves very well in it. An acquaintance commences. The stranger recommends himself more and more. An exchange of kind offices ensues. Gratitude and friendship succeed. Does not this seem very natural ? Is it not in perfect harmony with our benignant religion ?

Nations are composed of human creatures. *Gratitude* and *Friendship* take place between them, in much the same manner as between individuals, *with this remarkable difference* : The friendships between nations comprehend more valuable objects, than those between individuals, such as national peace, prosperity, liberty, and safety. The happiness of individuals is involved in these national blessings. Is it reasonable then to suppose, that the grander objects will have less influence than smaller ;

that is, that where the caufes are greater, the effects will be lefs? Befides, there may be a moft powerful cement between nations, by a mutuality of benefits; and this may be fo conftant, that the firft excitement by attention to *intereft*, as in other operations of the human mind, will grow up to an attachment of a higher kind, "*real good will*" towards one another. Who can deny this progreffion of the human mind? Who can bear to difapprove it? Who ought to difcourage it? This attachment will be more fpeedily, and more firmly eftablifhed, where the products of each nation are variant and yet peculiarly fuited to the other. *Then* the citizens of each are cheerfully employed at their refpective homes, in ufeful and agreeable labours for *themfelves* and their "*friends* and *allies*." This is a friendfhip founded on nature, promifing a permanency as lafting as the diftinctions between their foils and climates, and fuch as I am convinced the Author of Nature intended to take place among nations, when in his infinite wifdom he tho't proper to "*feparate* the children of men."

Far different is the cafe, when a nation "*ploughs* the waves," traffics over the globe, depends upon commerce for her ftrength and confequence, and exercifing all its arts, whatever they are, offers to us the collections made by her dexterity or violence, that fhe may draw to herfelf the profits of our induftry, and thus add to a power rendered by the fpirit and means of its elevation, already fufficiently imperative. "Such a nation," as a fagacious obferver of mankind has said, " *supremely jealous as to trade, t binds herself but little by treaties.**

The grants of such a nation, are manœuvres for obtaining ten fold, and it is very well for the other party if it is not ten thousand fold in return. *There is no just reciprocity in their contracts.* They exchange glass beads for gold dust and ivory.

FABIUS.

---

* *Montesquieu.*

LETTER XIV.

ANOTHER moſt powerful cement between nations is—their *reſemblance* of each other in forms of Government; more eſpecially, if that reſemblance is founded on the ſame endearing principle of *immediate derivation* from the governed, that is, from THE PEOPLE of each nation reſpectively. Then Man meets Man with a reciprocation of the kindlieſt diſpoſitions. It is private good will, operating through the character of citizenſhip: It is affection ſtrengthened by communication: It is the embrace of nations—and IF THEY HAVE COMMON SENSE OR ANY LOVE OF LIBERTY, this reſemblance becomes inveſted with irreſiſtible authority, when it *intereſtingly* diſcriminates between *them* and *monarchies* of other great nations. THIS is exactly and definitely the caſe of FRANCE AND THESE STATES, as contraſted with THE REST OF THE WORLD.

I appeal to the feelings of every heart not ſtone-dead to nature, whether——for *two perſons* or *nations* to be *unjuſtly* and *mortally* HATED —*for the ſame cauſe*—by *others, powerful in means* for gratifying their HATRED—is not a *ſtrong attraction* to UNION between *thoſe two perſons* or *nations* ? The propoſition although political, aſſumes nearly the force of a mathematical demonſtration: and, are we to be diverted from taking this ſalutary intimation, inſpired by Nature herſelf for our preſervation, this wholeſome, ſtrengthening nutriment, ſo ſuited to our

Conſtitutions, ſo cheap too, and ſo readily and ſo ſafely to be reached——that we may *feed* upon Ice-creams and Syllabubs, however delicately drugg'd or finely frothing from a dextrous hand?

Republics have always had THE HIGH HO-NOR OF BEING HATED BY *Monarchs,* tho' SOMETIMES COAXED BY THEM, in order to be rendered ſubſervient to their views: and THEY NEVER WERE HATED SO MUCH AS THEY ARE NOW.* If *France* ſhould not ſuc-

* * *

* *In the war of* our *revolution, almoſt all* Europe *favoured us.* Great-Britain *was thought too powerful and too haughty. Every great nation wiſhed her humiliation. Our diſtant wooden commonwealth, when compared with their ſtone-built pyramids of power, excited not the ſlighteſt apprehenſion.*

THE CASE IS NOW ENTIRELY CHANGED. *Since* France *has aboliſhed regal government, and has erected herſelf into a* Republic, *there is not an emperor, king, or prince, but who deteſts* republicaniſm *with an enmity never to be ſatiated but by its total deſtruction. If they can execute their will, not a ſucker, not the ſmalleſt twig of a root, from which the tree of liberty might grow up hereafter, will be left in the earth. The very ſoil will be dug up, and "ſifted as corn is ſifted in a ſieve," to diſcover and deſtroy all the ſeeds of happineſs.*

On the other hand, Great-Britain *has given ſuch indiſputable proofs of her* CONVERSION *to the modern orthodoxy in "religion and morality,"*

X

ceed in the prefent conteft, there is not an Elective Republic on Earth, that would not be immediately annihilated. Ours would be crufh'd at once—not under a *limited* Monarchy, fuch as we abrogated twenty years ago as intolerable, but under a *Defpotifm*: for the Queftion *now try-*

---

that fhe is clearly a confeffor, *and almoft a* martyr *in its holy crufade.*

She has fo fully manifefted her DEVOTION *to the caufe of* defpotifm *and fpoliation, that the crown'd* tyrants *and* robbers *now regard her as a bold, fturdy, and ritually-conjured accomplice, that may* be depended on *with unlimited confidence, for the execution of any project of profitable iniquity, provided fhe is admitted to a fhare.*

Let us now obferve, how regularly the plan for extinguifhing the light of liberty has been profecuted.

The United Provinces, *have by the arms of* Great-Britain *and* Pruffia *been for fome years declining into an arbitrary government.*

Republican Poland *was ftripped of one third of her provinces, by a confpiracy between* Ruffia, Auftria, *and* Pruffia.

No fooner did France *only difcover an* inclination *to be free, than all the great potentates roufed up with their ufual zeal at the lively call of* their " *religion and morality.*"

With-great cordiality it was RESOLVED, *that* France, *then in perfect* peace *with all of them— and her* king reigning in full poffeffion of his power—*fhould be feverely lopped all round. The mutilated form was then to be left to their* " *dear brother and coufin.*"

ing by combat, is—between *Republicanism* on one side, and *Despotism* on the other. ATTEND! ATTEND—with all the energies of your souls, my dear countrymen, to THIS MOMENTOUS TRUTH. The dagger of assassination is at the breast of *America;* and *France* alone holds back the hand that otherwise would strike it in—UP TO THE HILT.

————————————————————————

The embraces of their devout and virtuous ardor, were received with congenial feelings by "The empress of all the Russias." "Her majesty"—says *the holy and tranquilizing convention*—"*shall take upon herself* the INVASION of Poland," *&c.*

The duty thus devolved upon her, this faithful friend to "Humanity, and to the tranquility and welfare of Europe," *bloodily and piously performed; and in* 1794, *the catastrophe of* Polish *liberty closed, in a* PARTITION *of the whole republic between* Russia, Austria, *and* Prussia.

The further execution of the plan as it respected France, *was in the mean time going on; to end, it was fondly hoped, as the horrid aggression against* Poland *had just done, in* dismemberment *and* slavery.

Had this part of the plan succeeded, WE SHOULD HAVE BEEN LEFT ALONE. *Then all the resentment and execrations of the triumphant tyrants would have been directed against us, as the* original authors *of all the calamities of* Europe. *What the consequence would have been, he that runs may read.*

THANKS TO A GRACIOUS PROVIDENCE! *that on the plains of* Belgium, *and the mountains of* Italy, *it has been decided, that*—France *and* America *shall be free.*

Monarchs, *without exception*, think Republics reproachful to *their* government and dangerous to *their* authority. They abhor the PRINCIPLE on which they are founded; and the caufe of *defpotifm* has been much ftrengthened in this century, by the *acceffions* that have been made to *monarchies very great* before: A FACT, WORTHY OF OUR ATTENTION AND RE-MEMBRANCE.*

The Ancients ufed to comprefs a good deal of wifdom into fhort fentences. One of them was this—" Idem velle, ac idem nolle, id demum Amicitia eft"—" To agree in liking things, and to agree in difliking things, *that* is friendfhip."

Again I appeal to nature, to reafon, and to experience. Is it not a ftrong band?

Let us now attend to a comment upon it: Not a comment, where truth is obfcured by a cloud of words, or is fo cut to pieces by fub-

---

* *The great potentates of* Europe *have lately difcovered fuch ample advantages in their attention* " TO PUBLIC ORDER *and* GOOD GOVERNMENT"—*to borrow their favorite expreffions—by* joining together *to rob and fubjugate their weaker neighbours, adding their territories one after another to their own, that a few years ago it did not feem likely, that any limits could be put to the* MONSTROUS MASSES OF DESPOTIC POWER, *which they were continually rolling up. The republics of* France *and thefe* States *appear to be capable of becoming by their union and wifdom, the* PROTECTORS *of mankind, from the dangers impending over their heads.*

tle diſtinctions, that it is difficult for perſons who have not been uſed to ſuch operations, to redintegrate it: but to a comment, which amounts to an *exemplification* ſo important and extenſive, as to PROVE—what are the *genuine affections* of the human mind *on ſuch occaſions*.

Ancient *Greece* was divided into a number of States. *Athens* and *Sparta* were the great rivals for fame and power. Some of the other ſtates were ariſtocratical; and ſome of them demo-cratical. The government of *Sparta* was moſt favourable to ariſtocracy: that of *Athens* to democracy. In taking part in the wars between *Athens* and *Sparta*, the democratical ſtates al-ways ſided with the former, and the ariſtocrati-cal with the latter. So again, in controverſics between the democratical and ariſtocratical par-ties in the ſame ſlate, the other ſtates were al-ways inclined to one or the other, in correſ-pondence to the conformity of their principles reſpectively concerning thoſe ſeveral forms of government. When I ſay *always*, I mean, that theſe diſpoſitions were ſo general, that there were no exceptions ſufficient to weaken the ſtatement. I do not remember any; but I am bound to add—that I have ſome faint recollec-tion there was one, which was then thought very extraordinary.

Greece, we find, was ſplit into democratical and ariſtocratical parties. Theſe were main-tained with ſuch animoſity, that neither of them ever diſcovered, that MILDNESS AND MODERATION ARE LAWS OF OUR NATURE, that is, of our Maker, which never have been and never can be violated with impunity. To carry a point againſt their opponents was a triumph in which the ſhort-ſighted victors gloried. One point gained was a ſtep to another. The weaker party enraged by repeated injuries and inſults, called in foreign aid, firſt the *Perſians*, then the *Macedonians*, and at laſt, the *Romans*. After innumerable calamities, the democratical fury, and the ariſtocratical arrogance were melted down together, into one miſerable maſs of common ſlavery. Then at laſt they were quiet.

Thus alſo there was a conſtant and at length an inveterate controverſy between the ariſtocratical and the democratical parties of ancient *Rome*. Impotent of temper and blind to conſequences, they perſecuted each other till they were all together, by their own fatal activity, conſigned to the iron domination of as deteſtable miſcreants as ever bore the ſhape of man.

What is the LESSON which theſe examples hold out to us and to our allies, for both of us have parties reſembling thoſe that have been mentioned. If my weakneſs interprets rightly, it is this—that each party treat the other with juſtneſs and kindneſs as becomes brethren, "forbearing one another in love," and only, according to the apoſtle's uncommon and forcible expreſſion, "*provoking* to good works." ABOVE ALL THINGS, each party is to refrain from ſuch meaſures, as will inevitably tend to irritation.

The *danger* to republics from monarchies, and the *connection* to which republics are invited

by *the nature of things*, have been noticed.
France is fafe at all events.   She is fighting for
us as well as for herfelf, and we fhall be fafe
too, if we " know the things that belong unto
our peace," and " enfue" them : And it is to
be hoped, we fhall efcape the dreadful denunciation made to an infatuated people formerly
———"But now they are hid from thine eyes."
There is yet place for prudence and fecurity.

Let any difpaffionate man deliberately confider, whether there are any natural caufes at
prefent, or even remotely tending to a collifion
of interefts between *thefe States* and *France*.   I
am perfuaded he will not find any, but, DI-
RECTLY THE REVERSE. * Yet the loudeft
notes of alarm have been founded through our
land as if thofe interefls were IRRECONCILE-
ABLE, and that our beft welfare confifted in an
utter eftrangement.

It is not my intention now to treat of the
difgufts between us and *France*. They are not
the *natural products* of either country ; but political briars and thorns, the feeds of which have
been imported, and ftrange as it is, have been
raifed at a great expence—in hot-houfes.

Whatever blame may be caft on the *French
Nation*, on our fide provoking acts have been

---

* *After other far fuperior confiderations, may it
not be worth while to enquire—Whether* France
does not confume more of the fruits of our *foil than
any other nation ?   And alfo—whether* fhe *does
not fupply the only foreign raw material of extenfive
ufe in* thefe States.

committed. To acknowledge them would be noble. Some deem it more noble, if it is possible, to conceal them. They are therefore to be HID under invectives and resentments against *France*. For this purpose so many are straining their faculties and their voices : for, many are implicated. This circumstance engages their friends and adherents. Nor are there wanting excitements of another kind to heighten the clamor. If the *remembrance* of errors cannot otherwise be *obliterated*, let it be *confounded* among the tempestuous tumults of hostilities. If *France* can be slyly irritated into a declaration of war against us, or if we can be artfully wrought up to a proper degree of madness, and follow into a war those guides who have long since lost their way, *their* point is gained. Then *error* becomes *wisdom*, and *mischief* is dubbed *patriotism*.*

A friendly individual or a friendly nation may be of a warm temper. Slighter things from a supposed friend, will provoke more quickly and deeply than from another. In such cases, *consciousness of good will*, especially in seasons of

---

* " *If we are to judge by* reason *alone, it is the* interest *of a minister*, conscious of mismanagement, *that there should be a* war ; *because by a* war, the eyes of the public are diverted *from examining into* his conduct : *nor is he accountable for the bad success of a war, as he is for that of an* administration."

Speech of Sir Robert Walpole *in Parliament.*
Tind. *cont. of* Rapin's *Hist.* 20. 37.

great and perturbating diftrefs, will feel more keenly any appearance of unkindnefs. The friend is not to be loft, becaufe he is hafty, or in *the heat of combat for every thing dear to him,** through fufpicion of our expected affection, even injurious. An old proverb fays—"The falling out of lovers is the renewal of love." We certainly have been "Lovers," and if we are fallen out, let us make the experiment of reconciliation. The confequences will affect not only us, but our children, and the children of our children, and their children, to the lateft generations. We carry on *our* fhoulders the fame and fate of our nation.†

---

* " Res dura, *et* regni novitas *metalia* cogunt
" *Moliri*, *et* late *fines cuftode tueri*——
Virgil.

" *Againft my will—my fate*
" Surrounding dangers *and an* Infant State
" *Bid me* defend myfelf *with all my powers,*
" *And* guard with thefe feverities *my fhores.*"

† *When* Pericles, *one of the greateft men* Greece *ever produced, was diffuading* Tolmidas *a rafh man flufhed with former fuccefses, from attacking the* Beotians, *among other things which he faid, he ufed this* " memorable" *expreffion, as* Plutarch *calls it*——" *If thou wilt not take the advice of* Pericles, *wait for the advice of* TIME, *who is the* wifeft of all counfellors."

TOLMIDAS *would take the advice of neither; but was defeated, and killed with a multitude of the principal citizens.* " *Then* Pericles's *advice gain-*

Y

It is a mournful but inftructive ftudy, to read the hiftory of mankind. There we fee their follies and their vices depicted at full length, accompanied by their miferable attendants. The prominent feature is an aptitude to plunge into wars—

" For man too haughty in a profperous ftate
" Is blind, and heedlefs to his future fate."

A child may fet fire to a houfe, but a whole city may not be able to prevent the conflagration from levelling the buildings in every ftreet to the ground. " Ruunt omnes in fanguinem fuum populi—obftinatœque feritatis pœnas nunc fponte perfolvunt"——" ALL NATIONS RUSH FORWARD TO THE EFFUSION OF THEIR OWN BLOOD, AND VOLUNTARILY PAY THE PENALTIES OF THEIR OBSTINATE FIERCE-NESS."*

It is an obfervation of antiquity, that—*they* are *happy*, who grow *wife* by the misfortunes of *others*. This direction has been too little refpected ; and men generally chufe " to grow

---

ed him a high regard, together with great love and kindnefs from the people of Athens, *who looked upon him as a wife man, and a lover of his country."*

Plutarch's Life of Pericles.

* "Panegyr. Vet. Mamertinus *illuftrates the fact, by the example of* almoft all the nations of the world."

Gibb. *Hift.* ii. 108.

wife by *their own* misfortunes." But, as truth is never the worfe for being long neglected, I hope and truft, that my beloved countrymen will exert the good fenfe they eminently poffefs, and ftand upon the guard of PRUDENCE and AFFECTION for THEMSELVES and their POS-TERITY.

FABIUS.

LETTER XV.

IN the year 1728, the depredations of the *Spaniards* on the *British* commerce in the *European* and *American* seas, had been for a long time flagrant, extensive, cruel, and reproachful. The *British* nation was highly provoked.

The committee appointed by the House of Commons upon these depredations, after hearing all proper evidence, came on the fourteenth of *March*, to the following resolution, which being reported was agreed to by the house——— " That from the peace concluded at *Utrecht* in 1713. to this time, the *British* trade and navigation to and from the several *British* colonies in *America*, has been greatly interrupted by *continual* depredations from the *Spaniards*, who have seized very valuable effects, and have unjustly taken and made prize of *great numbers* of *British* ships and vessels in those parts, to the great loss and damage of the subjects of this kingdom, and in *manifest violation* of the treaties subsisting between the two crowns.*

The house then came to an unanimous resolution, that an address should be presented to the king, " desiring him to use his utmost endeavours, for preventing such depredations, procuring just and reasonable satisfaction for the losses sustained, and securing the free exercise of commerce and navigation."

---

* Tindal's *Cont. of* Rapin's *Hist. of* England, 20. 38.

Not long after, the bufinefs was taken up
again. " The minifter did not refufe to his
enemies in the houfe, any paper they could
call for, relating to the affairs between *Great-
Britain* and *Spain*, and the numbers they de-
manded were very great, and the time they
took up in reading. very long. At laft, the
grand committee, who continued moft affidu-
oufly to fit, upon the confideration of the
complaints againft the *Spanifh* depredations,
after long debates, refolved—" That feveral
fhips, merchandizes, and effects, belonging
to the merchants of this kingdom, trading to
Spain, *Portugal* and *Italy*, have been taken and
feized by the *Spaniards*, in *manifeft violation* of
the treaties fubfifting between the two crowns,
for which no reftitution has yet been made ; and
that the mafters and crews of feveral of the
faid fhips have been *barbaroufly* and *inhumanly*
treated."* An addrefs fimilar to the former
was voted and prefented.

In 1729, the famous treaty of *Seville* was
made. By the firft article, all former treaties
and conventions were confirmed. By the fecond, the two kings guaranteed each others
dominions. By the third, all engagements by
the treaty of *Vienna*, prejudicial to the treaties
between the two crowns, antecedent to the
year 1725, in which the treaty of *Vienna* was
made, were annulled. By the fourth, commerce was to be reftored to its former footing,
and orders were to be inftantly difpatched on all

---

* Tind *Cont.* 20. 41.

fides for that purpofe. By the fifth, the Ca-
tholic king obliged himfelf to make reparation
for all damages that had been done by his fubjects. By the fixth, commiffaries were to be
appointed on each part, to affemble at the
court of *Spain*, to examine and decide concerning fhips and effects taken at fea, to the time
fpecified in the preceding article—alfo, the
refpective pretenfions relating to abufes fuppofed to be committed, whether with refpect
to limits, or otherwife—and to make report
which fhould be executed. By the feventh,
commiffaries were to be appointed for deciding
all differences. By the eighth, the time for
the feveral commiffaries finifhing their com-
miffions, is limited to three years. The ninth,
tenth, eleventh, twelfth, thirteenth and fourteenth contained regulations, which it is needlefs to mention.*

However, the depredations ftill went on. In
1730, parliament was daily receiving petitions,
complaining of them. The commiffaries appointed by the king, in confequence of the
treaty of *Seville*, had not been able to prevail
on the court of *Madrid*, to name commiffaries
on the part of *Spain*, fo that not the fmalleft
progrefs was made in obtaining fatisfaction
for *Britifh* fubjects, and frefh complaints were
conftantly coming in. Every petition added
new matter for railing againft the minifter, Sir
Robert Walpole, afterwards earl of *Orford*, for
not declaring war, or at leaft iffuing orders for

---

* Tind. *Cont.* 20, 51.

reprifals. No man was ever more abufed. He was reprefented as a fool, a coward, a villain, and a traitor. The nation was raging for a war.

The minifter endeavoured to avoid it, and perfevered in his attempts to fettle the matters in variance, by negociation, being well affured, that this mode of proceeding would be much better for *Great-Britain*, than a war. A very great majority of the houfe of commons agreed with him in fentiment. It was accordingly refolved, that an addrefs fhould be prefented to the king, " defiring him to *continue* his endeavours to prevent depredations, to procure fatisfaction, and to fecure trade and navigation." The addrefs was prefented.*

In fucceeding years the depredations continued. Various refolutions were adopted in parliament, and feveral meafures propofed for relief.

In the courfe of the enquiries concerning thefe depredations from their commencement, it appeared, that many veffels trading fairly, with very valuable cargoes, and unqueftionably entitled to protection under the law of nations, and exifting treaties, were taken and confifcated, and frequently with a mockery of juftice, exhibiting the greateft contempt. The mafters and mariners were treated with the utmoft inhumanity and indignity. Their perfonal fufferings by loathfome imprifonment, or condemnation to hard labour, unwholefome food, iron

---

* Tind. *Cont.* 20, 95—20, 372.

fetters, and other atrocities, were enormous. One calamity they efcaped—they were not compelled to fight againſt their countrymen or allies.

In 1738, the houſe of commons, in an addreſs to the king, uſed this ſtrong language— "That before and ſince the execution of the treaty of *Seville*, and the declaration made by the crown of Spain, purſuant thereto, for the ſatisfaction and ſecurity of the commerce of *Great-Britain*, many unjuſt ſeizures and captures have been made, and great depredations committed by the *Spaniards*, which have been attended with many inſtances of *unheard of* cruelty and barbarity."

The miniſter was a man of ſpirit, and alſo of deliberation, qualities not often enough united. He was neither daring nor timid. His comprehenſive and informed genius gave him an elevation, from which, with enlightened ſerenity, he looked down upon the world of circumſtances, and preſided over conjunctures. He firmly adhered to his ſyſtem of peace and negociation.* He weighed and balanced things in his mind. He judged, that much reſpect was to be paid, to what would be thought

---

* *This great miniſter was adviſed by ſome of his friends, to tax the* Britiſh *colonies in* America. *He had the wiſdom and generoſity to reject that advice, obſerving that* Great-Britain *obtained ſufficient advantages from their commerce. Such advice was purſued ſome years afterwards, and the conſequences are well known.*

ABROAD, and that some regard was due even to the prejudices and mistakes of a power, whose friendship was essential to the welfare of his country : and *from some peculiarities in the state of European affairs*, he did not despair of accomplishing his purpose, unless it was defeated by her passions, so much to her benefit, that those who then blamed him, would afterwards approve his conduct.

After some time, preliminaries were signed as the basis of a treaty of accommodation. In consequence of these a convention was made. The court of *Spain* behaved improperly; and as her demands amounted to a claim of *perpetual right* to make seizures and captures *in time of peace*, on the same pretences that she had before acted upon, the nation was so inflamed, that in 1739, war began. In 1748, it ended, WITHOUT THE LEAST COMPENSATION WHATEVER BEING OBTAINED in the treaty of peace, for any of the PROPERTY the *Spaniards* had unjustly seized, or for any of the EXCESSES they had committed. War is a great burier.

Let us attend to what some years afterwards, calm and impartial *British* history says upon the subject.

" The main question for which the war was originally entered into, which was the commercial disputes between *Spain* and *Great-Britain* in the *West-Indies*, seemed to have been dropped, and mentioned in the treaty only for form sake, while each of those nations, though mutually weakened, found themselves in the

Z

very fame condition they were in before the war. THE SOBER, SENSIBLE PART OF THE PEOPLE OF ENGLAND, BEGAN NOW TO SPEAK WITH REVERENCE OF THE EARL OF ORFORD's PACIFIC ADMINISTRATION, AND THOSE WHO HAD BEEN HIS GREATEST ENEMIES, SEEMED AT A LOSS TO ACCOUNT FOR THE REASONS, WHY THE WAR HAD BEEN ENTERED INTO."*

What has been, now is, and in fucceeding ages will be the character of that man, with all perfons who are capable of forming a judgment of it ? *Chatham*, who had been one of his moft violent opponents, lived to difcern, and generoufly to acknowledge his fuperior merit. The excellent *Johnfon* ftyled him " a ftar of the firft magnitude ;" and it is apprehended, that it will be generally agreed, that he was one of the wifeft minifters that *his own country*, or any other ever had.

Look at *Britain* now ; and fee to what a condition fhe is brought, by being committed to the difpofal of minifters of a different character.

In defiance of all diffuading confiderations, in contempt of all energetic reclamations, her rulers courted a rupture with *France*. They obtained it. What with it ? In *Europe* and *America*, the deftruction of her brave foldiers and failors, by fword and peftilence—In *Africa*, the ruin of her fettlements—In *Afia*, her *Indian* empire tottering—affuredly to fall—Her bank,

*Tind. *Cont.* 21, 373, 374.

the fanctuary for filver and for gold, fhut—
Diftruft palfying her exertions—Confufion
catching her affairs from one to another, as a
contagion—her enemy " running upon her like
a giant"—and

" *Britain*, ocean's trident-bearing queen."

BRITAIN herfelf in imminent danger of
invafion.

It feems as if fome fin had been working at
the root of her full-blown profperity, for about
a quarter of a century.   Let us reflect.

We read in a book well worth reading, of
" the iniquity of a people being *full*," and
then of punifhment coming.

At the period alluded to, *Britain*, not innocent in other refpects, as weeping nations have
felt, then " put forth a hand" and profanely
touched *the ark of liberty*.   She drew it back
wounded and withered.   Not long afterwards,
the friend of mankind appeared within fight of
her fhores.   Uninftructed by her " *own misfortunes*," again fhe precipitated herfelf into the
fame violation of duty; unprovoked, quarrelled
with a people imitating the example of her
better days, refolved to be free, and even fup-
plicating her neutrality, when her compliance
with the equitable requeft, would have pene-
trated *France* with gratitude, and in all probability have faved the family for which fhe
pretended to arm.   She in her turn has fuppli-
cated, as vainly.

If it be confiftent with the providential government of the world, that another inftance
of divine difpleafure againft national abufes of
manifold and vaft bleffings be not, for a warning to others " *at which both the ears of every
one that heareth it fhall tingle,*" given in that
people, may heaven in mercy be gracioufly
pleafed to fave an offending yet generous nation,
from the madnefs of its governors. Perhaps,
" the place may be fpared for the righteous
that are therein"—for they are many.

Nor does *Britain* afford the only example of
the avenging calamities that appear in the
eftablifhed œconomy of human affairs, to be
bolted, and riveted on *Chriftian* nations particularly, who engage in fuch iniquitous enter-
prifes. I fay *Chriftian* nations, for as they
offend againft greater light, their guilt is more
glaring, and their punifhment more audaci-
oufly invoked. I fhall felect one more from
the roll of national crimes.

Spain, on fome part of whofe dominions,
it is boafted, that the fun is always fhining,
determined by every cruelty to extinguifh the
liberty of *The United Provinces*—a dot, that on
a map of the globe, muft be clofely fearched
for to be difcovered. *Spain* was then thick
clotted over with *American* gore. A dreadful
incumbrance !

The *dot* prevailed againft *the wide extended
realms* that fpread from the confines of the
arctic, to thofe of the antarctic circle, and
ftretched with belting longitude round both
hemifpheres. They fell, and—" Great was

the fall." The triumph over her by fo puny a foe, was beyond expreffion amazing. The hiftory of mankind could not fupply a parallel; and yet—another event took place, that diftanced the wonder.

THE MIGHTY POWER, " at which the world turned pale !"

funk—down—exhaufted—in the conteft. Soon afterwards, in the changeful courfe of human affairs, it implored and obtained the PROTEC-TION of the *little* people, which in *its* day of delufion, unconfcious of the *preferving* bleffing it ftrove to *deftroy*, it had doomed to perdition —againft a tyrannic conqueror, who in *his* day of delufion was infultingly " ftamping with his feet," upon its debilitated frame.

Let *us* be admonifhed by thefe tremendous examples.

Of *all improbabilities*, the eftablifhment of a republic in *France*, would fome few years ago have been judged *the moft improbable*. From *principle*, *magnitude*, and *connection*, it feems to announce a new feries of events on earth. " Secret things belong unto the LORD our GOD; but thofe things which are revealed belong unto us, and to our children forever."

The *French* are contending for the rights * granted to them by the charter of their CREA-

---

* *Nothing can be more evident or more infamous, than the* ambition *and* duplicity *with which the* combined powers *have acted in regard to* France.

TION.*(p 184) "Refrain from these men, and let them alone; for if this council, or this work be of men, it will come to nought: but, if it be of GOD, you cannot overthrow it; lest haply ye be found even to fight *against* GOD."

" *Towards the close of the summer of* 1791, *an extraordinary convention took place at* Pilnitz¶(1) *in* Saxony, *between the emperor* Leopold, *and the present king of* Prussia; *between whom, as principals, a treaty was formed, to which other powers are supposed to have afterwards acceded. The professed object of this treaty was sufficiently profligate and atrocious. It was the hostile invasion of* France *and the new modelling of its government. In his circular letter from* Pavia, *of the 6th of* July, *the emperor had avowed a similar intention, and had invited the princes of* Europe *to co-operate with him in the resistance to those principles so obnoxious to arbitrary authority, which had pervaded* France, *and which threatened to extend over the whole face of* Europe. *The league of* Pilnitz, *however, in which the empress of* Russia *is also to be considered as principally concerned, is generally supposed to have had more extensive views, and to have involved projects still more offensive, if possible, to the dictates of justice, and to the peace of* Europe. *The* PARTITION *of* France *as well as of* Poland, *or at least of a considerable portion of the territories of both, among the confederated powers, and a new modelling of the* Germanic *circles, are strongly suspected to have been the real principles upon which this infamous compact was founded. Dark and mysterious as the conduct of the allied courts has*

Our path is very plain. Let us not be inveigled from it, by a mean defire to cover *our own faults*, by the fanciful notions of a *political refinement*, or by an unjuftifiable rage for *fpeculations* upon the welfare of us and our pofterity. Let us affert and maintain OUR TRUE CHARACTER——*fincerity* of thought, and *rectitude*

---

been, relative to the fubftance of the conference, the imprudence of fome of the inferior agents has dropped occafional intimations which can leave little doubt of the criminality of their defigns. ¶ (2.)

" *Confidering, however, the convention of* Pilnitz *in the moft favourable point of view, and accepting the explanation of its exprefs framers, the proceeding is fufficiently unjuft and abfurd, to warrant the moft unqualified cenfure.* If any thing on earth is *facred, it is* the domeftic œconomy of both nations and individuals. *In private life the iniquity of interfering in a hoftile manner in the internal ftate of houfehold concerns of a neighbour, is felt and acknowledged by all mankind. Are then the rights of nations to be accounted lefs facred than thofe of private citizens? Are the lives of millions, who muft fall on both fides in fuch a conteft, of lefs confequence than the poverty or anxiety of individuals. But this is not the worft; the principle, if once admitted, is fubverfive of every right, and neceffarily fanctions every crime that can be committed againft fociety. It fanctions robbery and murder.*"

" France, *at the moment when this royal banditti were plotting againft her peace, might be faid literally to be in* a ftate of internal tranquility.

of action; and convince the world, that no man, or body of men, whatever advantages may for a while be taken of our unsuspecting

---

* *No* LANGUAGE CAN BE TOO STRONG, WHEN WE SPEAK OF THE RIGHT OF MAN TO LIBERTY.

Permit me to repeat, what above thirty years ago, before many of you whom I am now addressing, were born, I said to your fathers in the awful period, when the clouds that have since rained down so much blood on our land, were beginning to gather.

"*Kings or parliaments could not* give *the* rights essential to happiness, *as you confess those invaded by the stamp act to be. We claim them from a higher source*———*from* THE KING OF KINGS *and* LORD OF ALL THE EARTH. *They are not annexed to us by* parchments or seals. *They are* created *in us by the decrees of Providence, which establish the laws of our nature. They are* born *with us; and* cannot be taken *from us by any human power, without taking our lives. In short, they are founded on the immutable maxims of reason and justice. It would be an insult on the* DIVINE MAJESTY *to say, that* HE *has given or allowed any man or body of men* a right to make me miserable. *If no man or body of men has* such a right, *I have* a right to be happy. *If there can be no happiness without freedom, I have* a right to be free. *If I cannot enjoy freedom without security of property, I have* a right to be thus secured. *If my property cannot be secure, in case others, over whom I have no kind of influence, may take it from me by taxes, under pretence of public good,*

confidence, fhall ever be able to draw this nation out of the direct road of an open, candid, and generous conduct. The fun of truth will fooner or later diffipate the mifts of fallacy, and fhew things as they really are.

---

and for enforcing their demands, may fubject me to arbitrary, expenfive, and remote jurifdictions. I have an exclufive right *to lay taxes on my own property, either by myfelf, or thofe I can truft; of courfe to judge in fuch cafes of the public good; and to be exempt from fuch jurifdictions."*

An addrefs to the committee of correfpondence, &c. Philadelphia, 1776.

Many of the miferies that proceed from degradation to flavery, are visible. *Others more dreadful, are* invifible—*the vicious difpofitions generated in the tyrants and their fubjects. Beyond all, is that direful proftration of the Divine Image in man, which nations as well as individuals have experienced*——WHEN MEN LOSE EVEN THE DESIRE OF ACTING FROM THE IMPULSE OF THEIR OWN MINDS.

¶ (1) *The treaty of* Pavia *and that of* Pilnitz, *are fuppofed to be to—the fame purpofe.*

¶ (2) *The following paper, which has fince been made public, will ferve to unveil this myftery of* iniquity, *and cannot be read without indignation by any friend of liberty and juftice:*

Partition treaty between the courts in concert, concluded and figned at Pavia, in the month of July, 1791.

" *His majefty the emperor will retake all that* Louis *XVI.* conquered in the Auftrian Nether-

A a

We have nothing to do, but to quit the *new fangled philosophy* of imaginary vortices, and faithfully adhere to the *good old precepts* of common sense, and to the *sound dispositions* of human nature; with a noble and a pious faith to *believe*, that there are such things on earth as gratitude and friendship, *tho'* GOD *has* so formed men,

---

lands; *and uniting these provinces to the said* Netherlands, *will give them to his serene highness the* Elector Palatine, *so that these new possessions, added to the* Palatinate, *may hereafter have the name of* Austrasia.

" *Her serene highness the Arch-duchess* Maria Christina *shall be, jointly with his serene highness her nephew, the Arch-duke* Charles, *put into hereditary possession of the duchy of* Loraine.

" Alsace *shall be restored to the empire, and the bishop of* Strasburg, *as well as the chapter, shall recover their ancient privileges, and the ecclesiastical sovereigns of* Germany *shall do the same.*

" *If the* Swiss *cantons consent and accede to the coalition, it may be proposed to them to annex to the* Helvetic *league, the bishopric of* Parentrui, *the defiles of* Franche-Compte, *and even those of* Tyrol, *with the neighbouring bailiwicks, as well as the territory of* Versoy, *which intersects the* Pays de Vaud.

" *Should his majesty the king of* Sardinia *subscribe to the coalition,* la Bresse, la Bugey, *and the* Pays de Gex, *usurped by* France *from* Savoy, *shall be restored to him.*

" *In case his* Sardinian *majesty can make a grand diversion, he shall be suffered to take* Dau-

that they are influenced by a regard for their own interefts: in fhort to return to the wife and juft fentiments which we heretofore entertained for *thofe* who *firft* acknowledged our *independence*, and fet the bleffed example to

---

phiny *to belong to him for ever, as the neareft defcendant of the ancient dauphins.*

"*His majefty the king of* Spain *fhall have* Roufillon *and* Berne, *with the ifland of* Corfica, *and he fhall take poffeffion of the French part of* St. Domingo.

"*Her majefty the emprefs of all the* Ruffias *fhall take upon herfelf the invafion of* Poland, *and at the fame time retain* Kaminieck, *with that part of* Podolia *which borders on* Moldavia.

"*His majefty the emperor fhall oblige the* Porte *to give up* Choczim, *as well as the fmall forts of* Servia, *and thofe on the river* Lurna.

"*His majefty the king of* Pruffia, *by means of the above-mentioned invafion of the emprefs of all the* Ruffias *in* Poland, *fhall make an acquifition of* Thorn *and* Dantzic, *and there unite the* Palatinate *on the eaft, to the confines of* Silefia.

His majefty the king of Pruffia *fhall befides acquire* Luface, *and his ferene highnefs the elector of* Saxony *fhall in exchange receive the reft of* Poland, *and occupy the throne as hereditary fovereign.*

"*His majefty the prefent king of* Poland *fhall abdicate the throne, on receiving a fuitable annuity.*

"*His royal highnefs the elector of* Saxony *fhall give his daughter in marriage to his ferene highnefs the youngeft fon of his royal highnefs the grand duke*

others——*thofe* who nationally and individu-
ally, upon every occafion, through every period
of *our* conteft, uniformly and conftantly manifefted the moft affectionate attachment to us—
thofe, to whom under "A GRACIOUS PROVI-
DENCE," WE OWE our "*peace, liberty, and*

---

of all the Ruffias, *who will be the father of the
race of the hereditary kings of* Poland *and* Lithu-
ania.

(Signed)

　　　"*LEOPOLD,*
　　　" *PRINCE NASSAU,*
　　　" *COUNT FLORIDA BLANCA,*
　　　" *BISKHOFFSWERDER.*"

" *The king of* England *is faid to have acceded
to this treaty in* 1792: *And* Holland *to have acceded afterwards, provided the arrangements refpecting their limits with his imperial majefty fhall be
made according to the defire of the republic before
the partition.*

" *Spain renounced it when count* D'Aranda
*came into office as minifter, giving affurances how-
ever of the ftricteft neutrality.*" *How well that
neutrality has been obferved, following actions have
fhewn.*

" *In* 1793, *general* Dumourier *entered into an
agreement with the prince of* Saxe Cobourg, *commander of the forces of the combined powers,* " *to
co-operate in giving to* France *her conftitutional
king, and the conftitution fhe formed for herfelf.
On his word of honour, the prince pledged himfelf,
that he would not come upon the* French *territory to
make conquefts, but folely for the ends above*

safety," as we have *repeatedly* and *solemnly* DE-
CLARED TO ALL MANKIND——for ever to
renounce the deteſtable poſition, that we ought
to ſelect *them* out when ſurrounded by diſtreſs,

ſpecified." He *publiſhed a proclamation conform-*
able to this declaration.

Some few days afterwards, "A congreſs of the
repreſentatives of the combined powers was aſſembled
at Antwerp—*The duke of* York *and lord* Auck-
land *were preſent on the part of* Great-Britain.
The particulars of what paſſed on this important
occaſion, have not yet tranſpired——We only know,
that it was reſolved to commence a plan of active
operation againſt France. *The prince of* Cobourg
was compelled to unſay all that he had ſet forth with
ſo much ſolemnity, in his proclamation of the 5th—
and A SCHEME OF CONQUEST *was formally an-*
nounced in a new proclamation, which was iſſued
by the ſame general on the 9th of the ſame month."

" *It was obvious, that ſo impolitic a ſtep could*
have no other tendency, than to deſtroy all confidence
in the profeſſions of the allied powers."¶(3)

All their proceedings were directed by the ſame
inſidious and baſely ſelfiſh policy. " *If we obſerve*
the conduct," ſays an excellent Britiſh *writer,* "of
thoſe princes with reſpect to Poland, *it will afford*
the faireſt comment on their motives with reſpect to
France."¶(4)

They frequently publiſhed proclamations to deceive,
divide, and diſtract the French *nation, but all of*
them diſcordant and injurious. They never held
out a ſingle plan of accommodation. *While*
they were ſtriving to confound the public mind, they

and fighting the battles of freedom to be the firſt objects, againſt whom we are to exert THAT VERY SOVEREIGN POWER THEY WERE IN-STRUMENTAL in conferring upon us ; the *firſt* people, into whoſe hearts we are to plunge

---

ſteadily and invariably purſued their original deſign of DISMEMBERING *the kingdom, and then eſtab-liſhing a* DESPOTIC MONARCHY *upon its wretched debris.*

¶(3) New Annual Regiſter *for* 1793, *page* 165, *&c.*

¶(4) New Annual Regiſter *for* 1792, *p.* 120.

Since theſe letters were firſt publiſhed, a trea-tiſe called " The Political State of *Europe* at the beginning of 1796," has been received.

The author, *Calonne*, late miniſter of the finances of *France*, under LEWIS XVI. whoſe hopes entirely reſt on the reſtoration of monar-chy, a writer of extenſive information and emi-nent talents, a vehement enemy of *French* repub-licaniſm, and as warm a friend to the coaleſced powers, aſcribes the bad ſucceſs of their mea-ſures to the weakly—ſelfiſh, cruel and provoking outrages of the confederates. He employs many pages on this ſubject. The following quotation may be ſufficient to ſhew the iniquity of their proceedings : It is from that part which he entitles——" INTENTIONS THAT WERE MANIFESTED."

" We ſhall not heſitate to diſcloſe what no pains have been taken to conceal : A throne was to be *re-eſtabliſhed*, and its fall has diffuſed

THOSE VERY SWORDS THAT BY THEIR AID AT THE EXPENCE OF THEIR BLOOD AND THEIR TREASURE have been put into our hands. HEAVEN FORBID! that *American gratitude* fhould become a by-word among civilized nations to the lateft ages, emphatically to de-

---

an apparent *fatisfaction*; an *oftentatious defire* was fhewn of *retrieving*, but foon was evinced *the manifeft purpofe of* DISMEMBERING *the empire*; thofe who announced themfelves as auxiliaries, foon behaved as *invaders*; oppreffion was to be oppofed, and *unblufhing examples* of it were given; the world was fcandalized by a *ferocious rapacity*, when it was of fo much importance that it fhould be edified by fingular acts of juftice; and a war, which ought to have been a war of *general intereft*, of *honour*, and *generofity*, is become a war of AGGRANDIZEMENT, SELFISHNESS, and ILLIBERAL VIEWS.

" We cannot be accufed of exaggerating what we fhould *wifh to palliate*; or of arraigning, by rafh fuppofitions, the various intentions of the cabinets of *Europe:* we only fpeak of appearances: of appearances that have manifefted themfelves to *every underftanding* by facts of *public notoriety*; firft, by *equivocal proclamations*, whofe *ever-varying complexion* betrayed *a purpofe very different* from their oftenfible fpirit; and where the words of PLEDGE and INDEMNITY but imperfectly veiled *more extended views*; afterwards by the taking of *Valenciennes* in the name of the emperor, and by the union of *Con-*

fcribe that fupremacy of depravity, which no other terms can fully define. Then, indeed, it may be fome confolation to our darkened and perverted minds, that *"punic faith"* will be its allied companion.

FABIUS.

---

fica to the *Britifh* empire, which, in whatever manner it was effected, has rendered the difin- tereftednefs of *England* as fufpicious as that of the other powers." *Page* 19.

This is the language of a man, who for feveral years has been exerting his utmoft efforts to promote the eftablifhment of monarchical government in *France*, by the interference of the combined powers. What lefs than *truth*, evident to *"every underftanding,"* could have induced him to hold fuch language?

[*A* NOTE *for* LETTER IV.]

It does not appear neceſſary to undertake the laborious and afflictive employment of deſcribing the dreadful maſs of miſeries that conſtantly preyed on the poorer claſſes of the people in France, *under the old government.*

Let the following extracts from the ingenious, truly philoſophical, benevolent, and pious Saint Pierre, *author of the celebrated* "Studies of Nature,"* *ſuffice.*

"The diſtrict of *Caux* is the moſt fertile country in the World. Agriculture, on the grea, ſcale, is there carried to the height of perfection. The deepneſs of the ſoil, which, in ſome places, extends to five and ſix feet ; the manure ſupplied from the ſtratum of marl over which it is raiſed, and that of the marine plants on its ſhores, which are ſpread over its ſurface, concur toward clothing it with the nobleſt vegetables.—

---

* This work was publiſhed in *France*, ſeveral years before the revolution.

" It is a ſingular phenomenon in the hiſtory of the preſent period, that the author of " *Studies of Nature*," the profeſſed panegyriſt and penſioner of *Louis* XVI. ſhould be careſſed, ſhould be reſpected, ſhould be promoted to honour by that very national convention, which dethroned and decapitated his patron and benefactor. Can a ſtronger teſtimony be borne to wiſdom and virtue !"———Preface to the tranſlation, by *Henry Hunter*, D. D. miniſter of the *Scots* church, *London.*

B b

"I happened one day to be walking through this
fine country ; and admired, as I went, its plains
fo well cultivated, and fo extenfive, that the eye
lofes itfelf in the unbounded profpect. Their
long ridges of corn, humouring the undulations
of the ground and terminating only in villages,
and caftles furrounded with venerable trees, prefented the appearance of a Sea of verdure, with
here and there an ifland rifing out of the Hori-
zon. It was in the month of March, and very
early in the morning. It blew extremely cold
from North-eaft. I perceived fomething red
running acrofs the fields, at fome diftance, and
making toward the great road, about a quarter
of a league before me. I quickened my pace,
and got up in time enough to fee they were two
little girls in red jackets and wooden fhoes, who,
with much difficulty, were fcrambling through
the ditch which bounded the 1oad. The talleft,
who might be about fix or feven years old, was
crying bitterly. " Child," faid I to her, " what
" makes you cry, and whither are you going at
" fo early an hour ?" " Sir," replied fhe, " my
" poor mother is very ill. There is not a mefs
" of broth in the whole parifh. We are going
" to that church in the bottom, to try if the
" Curè of this parifh can find us fome. I am
" crying becaufe my little fifter is not able to
" walk any farther." As fhe fpake, fhe wiped
her eyes with a bit of canvas, which ferved her
for a petticoat. On her raifing up the rag to her
face, I could perceive that fhe had not the fem-
blance of a fhift. *The abject mifery* of thefe
children, fo poor, *in the midft of plains fo*

fruitful, wrung my heart. The relief which I could adminifter to them was fmall indeed. I myfelf was then on my way to fee mifery in other forms.

" The number of wretches is fo great, in the beft cantons of this province, that they amount to a *fourth,* nay, to a *third* of the inhabitants in *every parifh.* The evil is continually on the *increafe.* Thefe obfervations are founded on my perfonal experience, and on the teftimony of many parifh-minifters of undoubted veracity. Some Lords of the Manor order a diftribution of bread to be made, once a week, to moft of their peafantry, to *eke out their livelihood.* Ye ftewards of the public, reflect that *Normandy* is the richeft of our provinces; and extend your calculations, and your proportions, to *the reft of the kingdom !*——

" *Picardy, Britany,* and *other provinces,* are INCOMPARABLY MORE TO BE PITIED than *Normandy.* If there be twenty-one millions of perfons in France, as is alledged, there muft be then, at leaft SEVEN MILLIONS OF PAUPERS.——

" The wretchednefs of the lower orders is the principal fource of our phyfical and moral maladies.

Vol. 2. *page* 98—114.

" The perfons who difcover, and who unveil the evils under which their country labours, are not the enemies which·fhe has to fear; the perfons who flatter her, they are her real enemies.——

" As far as I am concerned, I fhould believe that I had already deferved well of my country, had I only announced in her ear this awful truth : That fhe contains in her bofom more than SEVEN MILLIONS OF POOR, and that their number has been proceeding in an *increaf-ing* proportion, from year to year, ever fince the age of *Louis* XVI.

"God forbid ! that I fhould wifh or attempt to difturb, much lefs deftroy, the different orders of the State. I would only wifh to bring them back to the fpirit of their natural inftitution. Would to God that the clergy would endeavour to merit, by their virtues, the firft place, which has been granted to the facred-nefs of their functions; that the nobility would give their protection to the citizens, and render themfelves formidable only to the enemies of the people ; that the adminiftrators of finance, directing the treafures of the public to flow in the channels of agriculture and commerce, would lay open to merit the road which leads to all ufeful and honourable employment ; that every woman, exempted, by the feeblenefs of her conftitution, from moft of the burthens of fociety, would occupy herfelf in fulfilling the duties of her gentle deftination, thofe of wife and mother, and thus cementing the felicity of one family ; that, invefted with grace and beauty, fhe would confider herfelf as one flower in that wreath of delight, by which Nature has attached man to life; and while fhe proved a joy and a crown to her hufband in particular, the complete chain of her fex might indiffolubly compact all the other bonds of national felicity.

" THE PEOPLE fupports, without any return on my part, the weight of my exiftence : it is ftill much worfe when they are loaded with the additional burthen of my irregularities. To them I ftand accountable for my vices and my virtues, more than to the magiftrate. Befides, religion lays me under an exprefs injunction to love them. When fhe commands me to love men, it is THE PEOPLE fhe recommends to me, and not the great: to *them* fhe attaches all the powers of fociety, which exift only *by them*, and *for them*. Of a far different fpirit from that of modern politics, which prefent *nations* to kings as *their domains*, fhe prefents kings to nations, as their fathers and defenders. THE PEOPLE WERE NOT MADE FOR KINGS, BUT KINGS FOR THE PEOPLE. I am bound therefore, I who am nothing, and who can do nothing, to contribute my warmeft wifhes, at leaft, towards their felicity.

" Farther, I feel myfelf conftrained, in juftice to the commonalty of our own country, to declare, that I know none in *Europe* fuperior to them in point of generofity, though, liberty excepted, they are THE MOST MISERABLE of all with whom I have had an opportunity to be acquainted. Did time permit, I could produce inftances innumerable of their *beneficence*.

" I have remarked, for example, that many of our inferior fhop-keepers fell their wares at a lower price to the poor man than to the rich ; and when I afked the reafon, the reply was, " Sir, every body muft live." I have likewife obferved, that a great many of the lower order never haggle, when they are buying from poor people like themfelves : " Every one," fay they, " muft live by his trade." I faw a little child, one day, buying greens from a herb-woman : fhe filled a large apron with the articles which he wanted, and took a penny : on my expreffing furprize at the quantity which fhe had given him, fhe faid to me, " I would not, Sir, have given fo much to a grown perfon ; but, I would not for the world take advantage of a child." I knew a man of the name of *Chriftal*, in the *rue de la Magdelaine*, whofe trade was to go about felling Auvergne-waters, and who fup-ported for five months, *gratis*, an upholfterer, of whom he had no knowledge, and whom a law-fuit had brought to *Paris*, becaufe, as he told me, that poor upholfterer, the whole length of the road, in a public carriage, had, from time to time, given an arm to his fick wife. That fame man had a fon eighteen years old, a paralytic and changeling from his birth, whom he maintained with the tendereft attachment, without once confenting to his admiffion into the hofpital of incurables, though frequently folicited to that effect, by perfons who had intereft fufficient to procure it : " God," faid he to me, " has given me the poor youth : it is my duty to take care of him." I have no doubt that he ftill continues to fupport him, though he is under the neceffity of feeding him with his own hands, and has the farther charge of a frequently ailing wife.

" I fhould never have done, were I to indulge myfelf in detailing anecdotes of this fort.* They would be found worthy of the admiration of the rich, were they extracted from the hiftory of favages, or from that of the Roman emperors ; were they two thoufand years old, or had they taken place two thoufand leagues off. They would amufe their imagination, and tranquilize their avarice. *Our own commonalty undoubtedly, well deferves to be loved.* I am able to demonftrate, that their moral goodnefs is the firmeft fupport of government, and that, notwithftanding their own neceffities, to them our foldiery is indebted for the fupple-

---

The following inftance of benevolence cannot be too much commended. It took place on capt. Thurot's attack on Carrickfergus, in Ireland, in the year 1760.

" One circumftance that attended this difpute, deferves to be tranfmitted to pofterity, as an inftance of that courage, mingled with humanity, which conftitutes true heroifm. While the *French* and *Englifh* were hotly engaged in one of the ftreets, a little child ran playfully between them, having no idea of the danger to which it was expofed : *a common foldier of the enemy*, perceiving the life of this poor innocent at ftake, grounded his piece, advanced deliberately between the lines of fire, took up the child in his arms, conveyed it to a place of fafety ; then returned to his own place, refumed his mufket, and renewed his hoftility."

Smollett's *Cont. of the Hiftory of England, Vol.* 3, *page* 392.

ment to their miferable pittance of pay, and
that to them the innumerable poor with whom
the kingdom fwarms, owe a fubfiftence wrung
from penury itfelf.

"SALUS POPULI SUPREMA LEX ESTO, faid
the ancients: let the fafety of the people be
the paramount law, becaufe their mifery is the
general mifery. This axiom ought to be fo
much the more facred in the eyes of legiflators
and reformers, that no law can be of long duration, and no plan of reform reduced into
effect, unlefs THE HAPPINESS OF THE PEOPLE
is previoufly fecured. Out of their miferies
abufes arife, are kept up, and are renewed.———

"CRIMES SPRING UP ONLY FROM THE
EXTREMES OF INDIGENCE AND OPULENCE.

" Immenfe landed property is ftill more injurious than that of money and of employments,
becaufe it deprives the other citizens, at once,
of the focial and of the natural patriotifm.
Befides, it comes, in procefs of time, into
the poffeffion of thofe who have the employments and the money ; it reduces all the fubjects
of the State to dependance upon them, and
leaves them no refource for fubfiftence but the
cruel alternative, of degrading themfelves by
a bafe flattery of the paffions of thofe who have
got all the power and wealth in their hands, or
of going into exile. Thefe three caufes combined, the laft efpecially, precipitated the ruin
of the *Roman* empire, from the reign of *Trajan*,
as *Pliny* has very juftly remarked. They have
already banifhed from *France* more fubjects
than the revocation of the edict of *Nantes* did.

When I was in *Pruffia*, in the year 1765, of
the hundred and fifty thousand regular troops
which the king then maintained, a full third
was computed to confift of *French* deferters.
I by no means confider that number as exag-
gerated, for I myfelf remarked, that all the
foldiers on guard, wherever I paffed, were
compofed, to a third at leaft, of *Frenchmen*;
and fuch guards are to be found at the gates of
all the cities, and in all the villages on the great
road, efpecially toward the frontier.

"When I was in the *Ruffian* fervice, they
reckoned near three thoufand teachers of language of our nation in the city of *Mofcow*,
among whom I knew a great many perfons of
refpectable families, advocates, young eccle-
fiaftics, gentlemen, and even officers. *Germany* is filled with our wretched compatriots."

Vol. 4. 99–119.

Such has been *the deplorable ftate of that moft
fertile country,* France, *for ages paft. Its government has been in conftant counteraction to the
bleffings beftowed upon it by Heaven. But—there
is a* REACTION *in the operations of injuftice and
cruelty, the remarkable inftances of which demonftrate how much fafer, if better principles do not
perfuade, it is to be* benefactors *than* oppreffors.

" Delightful land! Ah, now with general voice,
" Thy village fons and daughters may rejoice,
" Thy happy peafant now no more, a flave
" Forbad to tafte one good that NATURE gave,
" Views with the anguifh of indignant pain
" The bounteous harveft *fpread for him in vain.*
" *Oppreffion's* cruel hand fhall dare no more
" To feize with iron gripe his fcanty ftore,
"And from his famifh'd infants wring thofe fpoils,
" The hard-earn'd produce of his ufeful toils:
" For NOW, on *Gallia's* plain the peafant knows
" Thofe *equal rights* impartial HEAV'N beftows.
" He now by freedom's ray illumin'd, taught
" Some felf-refpect, fome energy of thought,
" Difcerns the bleffings *that to all belong,*
" And lives to *guard* his humble fhed from wrong.

F I N I S.

ERRATA.

In Page 22, for "*confideration*," read "confederation."

42, for "*power*," read "authority."

ib. for "*fpeculations*" read "expectations."

51, for "*landing*" read "landed."

57, for "*Phlyarzrians*" read "Phlyazians."

66, for "*they anfwered*," read "it is anfwered."

78, for "*now more than*" read "now than."

103, for "*nature fhrinks*" read "natures fhrink."

125, for "*Bofom*" read "Befom."

160, for "*communication*" read "communion."

CPSIA information can be obtained at www.ICGtesting.com
Printed in the USA
BVOW06s1117201013

334199BV00004B/22/P